THE HISTO

THE HISTORY OF PORT TALBOT

with photographs

SALLY ROBERTS JONES

Goldleaf Publishing
Port Talbot

Printed in Great Britain by
John Penry Press, Swansea

Foreword

A complete list of all the books and articles used in writing this history of Aberafan/Port Talbot would be almost as long as the history itself. However, the main sources used have been *Old Afan and Margam* by James O'Brien, *The Story of Taibach and District* by A. Leslie Evans, *Profile of a Welsh Town* by J. Ivor Hanson, the *Transactions of the Aberafan and District Historical Society, 1928-1932* and the *Transactions of the Port Talbot Historical Society, 1963* to date.

I would like to express my thanks to all my friends and fellow members of Port Talbot Historical Society, and in particular to Messrs. A. Leslie Evans, A. Rees, J.V. Hughes, G. Lahive, A.J. Vollans and D. John Adams, without whom this history could not have been written. And I must also acknowledge the long-term support received from West Glamorgan Library Service, which has been much appreciated.

S.R.J.

Chapter 1

The Beginning

According to an ancient legend, the present Aberafan is the third town of that name, and there have been two others, each of them built farther out towards the sea. Both of them are now lost, either under the sand or under the waves of the Bristol channel.

This may be more than a legend. To begin with, many centuries ago the Bristol channel did not exist, and a much smaller river Severn ran through a broad, fertile valley, to join the sea somewhere out beyond what is now Gower. Birch trees grew along the river banks and even today chunks of wood from what was once Coed Arian (Silver Wood) wash up on the shore, mute evidence of vanished forests. It is quite possible that somewhere on the slopes of that long-vanished Lower Severn Valley, the first 'Bravonites' built their huts and chased the deer.

There is no evidence of that first settlement, if there was one, no foundations of huts, or pottery, or even a rubbish tip; but when we come to the second Aberafan we do have just a few clues to suggest that it did exist. Most of these were found in 1835-6 when the Docks were built and the course of the river Afan was straightened so that it flowed directly into the sea instead of looping round to join the Ffrwdwyllt in Taibach; more evidence was uncovered in 1896 when the Docks were extended. In those days archaeology hardly existed as a science, and there were no heritage trusts to rescue any 'finds'; what little we know, we owe chiefly to C.R.M. Talbot of Margam castle who described the discoveries in a letter to his friend, L.W. Dillwyn of Penllergaer.

'Yesterday I found at the harbour, Port Talbot, about 25 feet below high water mark, a brass spear head about nine inches long, many stags' antlers, a large brass coin of Commodus, several pairs of old fashioned leathern shoes, foundations of buildings, footmarks of deer and oxen; and old fences in a state of carbonization have been found near the same place, at various depths, from five to twenty feet below the present high water level, also an ancient sea wall having behind it well marked indications of cultivation by ridge and furrow, which could not now keep out the present water by several feet.'

The Rev. H.H. Knight, vicar of Neath, added a little more to this in a letter published in 1859; he referred to the finding of a 'druid circle', a key, human bones, and two coffins containing skeletons, most of these things being either Roman or early mediaeval in date. The number of human bones discovered is probably due to the fact that there was an ancient burial ground in this area, known as 'Platch yr Eglwys' or 'Plattau yr Hen Eglwys'; the 'old church' referred to must have existed before St. Mary's Church was built and it may have been the vanished church of St. Thomas. It seems that at the end of the last century many pieces of coloured glass were found in the sand in that area, perhaps from a window.

(Curiously enough, Aberafan is still moving inland; after the great flood of 1768, for instance, Aberafan Bridge was rebuilt a little higher up the river to avoid any danger of it being swept away by flooding, and more recently the new Civic Centre has followed the pattern; when the East Bank development is completed, the commercial centre of the town will have moved again too.)

The first people to live in the Aberafan area would have been what are known as 'hunter gatherers', small wandering family groups who lived on whatever they could collect or trap: shellfish, berries, roots, perhaps the occasional deer or goat. There is evidence of such people camping at Merthyr Mawr, but in our own district the earliest definite trace of habitation is a stone axe, found on Aberafan beach in January 1970, which still had part of its wooden handle; it has been dated to c.4000 B.C. – almost twice as old as Stonehenge. The axe is made of Cornish gabbro, and bears witness to trade between South Wales and the West Country as much as 6000 years ago. (A similar axe, this time without its handle, was found on the same part of the beach a few months later.)

We know very little about these people of the New Stone Age, but since such axes were used for felling trees, clearing undergrowth and for cultivating crops, it is possible that the axes belonged to some of the earliest farmers in Aberafan.

However, though the axe-makers were very highly skilled at working stone, their material had its limitations, and by 1400 B.C. stone had been replaced in many cases by bronze, for both tools and weapons. An axe, of course, could be both, and several bronze axes have been found on Morfa Beach dating from this time, some 3500 years ago.

After bronze came iron, a much tougher material, and with iron came the people we know as the Celts, and a language which was the ancestor of modern Welsh. However, though the Celts seem to have been more aggressive and warlike than the people before them, they were not all-conquering invaders; for instance there are still words in both Welsh and English which are derived from the language spoken by the earlier settlers, and it is quite possible that somewhere in Port Talbot today there live descendants of the man or woman who once used the stone axe found on Aberafan Beach.

The Celts who settled in South Wales were known as the Silures. Like all Celts they were great lovers of songs and stories, and fine craftsmen who produced beautiful things in stone and metal. Although their chieftains were warlike, they seem to have treated war almost as a game, with its own strict rules of honour, and the ordinary people, farmers, metalworkers, weavers and the like were probably able to get on with their lives without too much disruption while the more aggressive young men rode off on cattle raids or attacks on a neighbouring group of warriors.

The houses these people would have lived in would have looked very primitive to us; their round stone walls, often only three or four feet high, were roofed with branches and turf, and there were no chimneys or stone floors, or even furniture as we know it. In times of serious danger the whole tribe would take shelter in a hill-fort, a hilltop strongpoint defended by banks and ditches of earth and stone, and equipped with a well or other water supply, and stand siege there until the weather or lack of supplies forced the enemy to go away. There are a number of these strongholds on the hills above Aberafan. (Since the lower land tended to be either marshy or heavily wooded, more people lived on high ground in those days in any case.)

Then in A.D. 43, the Roman army landed in Britain. The

A Celtic farmstead, circa 50 A.D.

(David West)

Romans had come to Britain almost a hundred years before, when Julius Caesar sailed across the Channel, but this time they were determined not to be driven off. (Although Caesar reported back to Rome that he had conquered the island, his report was largely propaganda, and his visit made very little difference to the Britons.) Like most invading forces, the Roman legions conquered the south-east of Britain with very little difficulty, but when they came up against the Silures in South Wales it was quite another matter, and there was a long, hard struggle before Rome was able to drive her roads across the mountains and valleys towards the rich pastures and gold mines of the West.

Once the legions began their road-building programme, however, Aberafan soon found itself on the main coast road to West Wales. This was known as the Via Julia Maritima (i.e. 'the seaside road built by Julius Frontinus') and a number of Roman milestones have been found locally, particularly two which were excavated in the dock area c.1846, one commemorating the Emperors Diocletian and Gordianus, and the other Emperor Maximinus. It was the Roman custom to have forts or 'stations' at fixed distances along these roads; Cardiff was one of these, and Neath another, as was Loughor, while 'Bovium' was probably near Cowbridge, and a fifth, not yet traced, seems to have been in the Pyle/Margam area. However, though Aberafan does not seem to have been the site of any Roman military settlement, there was evidently a noticeable Roman presence in the area, and a number of coins and 'Roman remains' were found in the Docks excavations of 1846.

(The finest of these Roman finds so far, turned up on Margam beach, on September 9th, 1990, when Mr. G. Lahive found a coin dating from 77 A.D., in the reign of Titus Caesar. It is a brass sestertius in remarkably good condition).

We know very little about the effects of the Roman conquest of Britain on South Wales. At one time it was believed that the Romans simply built four forts, one at each corner of Wales – Caerleon, Carmarthen, Caernarfon and Chester – in order to prevent any uprisings, and then left the natives to look after themselves, but recent archaeological excavations suggest that there were Roman civilians as well as soldiers in Wales, and through them our ancestors would have had access to

Roman technical knowledge in a variety of areas, from architecture and civil engineering to improved methods of making glass. And not only were these skills available but the Britons were encouraged to learn about them; Agricola, who was the Roman governor of Britain from 77-84 A.D., took the sons of the British chieftains and saw that they were trained in all the ways of Roman civilisation – baths, banquets, the liberal arts, the building of public squares and grand temples. Eventually the brainwashed princelings came to wear the Roman toga in place of their native trousers, shave off their drooping moustaches, and speak Latin by choice.

If it existed at all at that time, then Aberafan was only a cluster of small huts at the crossing point of the river Afan; there would have been no grand public baths, and probably no toga-clad chieftains here – though it is quite possible that the local people had picked up enough Latin to make themselves understood, just as their descendants would one day pick up the English language. The ordinary tribesmen would have marched about in trousers and a tunic made of checked cloth, would very probably have been heavily tattooed, and would have spoken a language that was not yet quite the Welsh that we know. (The Romans did not think of women as important, so we know less about them, but from characters like Boudicca and the treacherous Queen Cartimandua, we know that British women were quite equal to their menfolk!)

The Romans had destroyed the Druids, who had been the priests, lawgivers and doctors of the Britons, but the native British were still allowed to worship their own gods, beings like Lludd (from whom we get Ludgate and probably Londinium), Rhiannon the mother goddess (who is perhaps under another name, the 'Mari' of the Mari Lwyd custom), or Cernunnos, the horned god of the forests. They worshipped especially at pools and fountains, like Ffynnon Pantyrarian at Baglan, and celebrated the important seasons of the year with bonfires and special ceremonies, reading the future in the flight of birds or the opening of leaves on the trees.

And as they went about the daily work of caring for their cattle, ploughing and sowing and reaping, or perhaps fishing out in the bay, the people would have seen the Roman legions and their messengers passing east and west along the Via Julia

Maritima, on their way to drive off Irish raiders or escort the gold trains from the mines of Dolau Cothi on their way to the Emperor's money-chests in Rome. Then, in the evenings, when the doors of their huts were barred against the terrors of darkness, they would listen to wandering storytellers and poets who would remind them of the glories of the days before the legions came, and tell tales of heroes like the giant Bran and his beautiful sister Branwen. After a while there might be new faces in the village – veterans who had served their time with the legions, and settled down with their British wives and half-British children in their adopted country.

The legions stayed in Britain for almost 400 years, and then left, bag and baggage, called back to Rome to defend it against barbarian attackers. The Britons were left to defend themselves against invaders from all sides – Irish raiders, Picts in Scotland, Angles, Saxons and Jutes from the Continent, and the Vikings who gave their names to Swansea (Sweyn's Island) and many other places on the Glamorgan coast.

There are no written records from these centuries, and we can only guess at what life was like for the ordinary people of Aberafan. By now Britain had been converted to Christianity, and the large number of carved memorial stones found in the area suggest that there was a monastery, or at least a Christian community, at Margam. From the stones we learn the names of some of those early natives of Port Talbot: Bodvoc, Catotigirnus his father, Eternalis Vedomavus his great-grandfather (perhaps one of the Roman soldiers who settled in Wales on retirement), Pumpeius Carantorius, Cantusus and his son Paulinus, Cynfelin (whose memorial cross featured on a postage stamp some years ago). They worshipped in tiny churches – St. Baglan's, from which Baglan gets its name, founded by a missionary from Llantwit Major; St. Cyfelach's, in the Docks area; St. Non's at what is now Eglwys Nunydd – but when their children were sick, they still took them to Pantyrarian to be healed of their rickets, or called on the old Celtic gods (now disguised as Christian saints, like St. Brigid) to cure them.

As for daily life, they were pastoral farmers; they grew corn and vegetables for their own needs, and bacon was an important part of their diet, but their main 'crops' were their

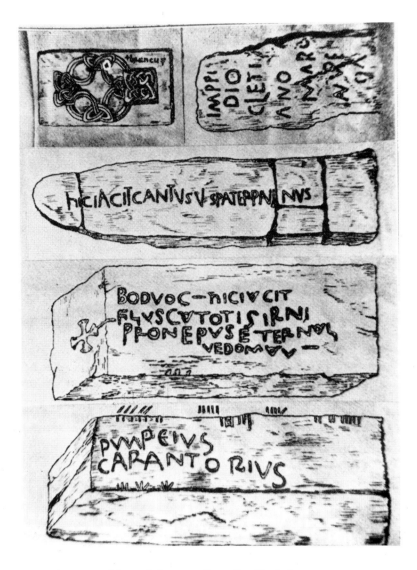

Memorial stones from the Dark Ages

sheep and cattle. In winter they lived down in the valleys, tucked away from blizzards and harsh winds, but in the summer the younger people would take the flocks and herds up to the high ground and stay there until the storms of autumn drove them down to the lowlands again. We can still see this yearly migration reflected in place names: Hendre, the old or main settlement where they spent the winter (sometimes it was called Gaeaf-tre, or Goytre, the winter settlement); in the summer they lived at the 'hafod' or 'summer place'.

It was a hard life, but one with its own pleasures and its own excitements, especially at the time of the great celebrations like Christmas and May Day, St. John's Eve and Hallowe'en, when there were bonfires and feasting and fortune-telling. The Church might have Christianised all these things, but there would have been very little difference between the life of a family from Aberafan in 1050 and their ancestors a thousand years before.

Chapter 2

The Lords of Afan

In the eleventh century Wales and England were two distinct countries, and even if, in 1066, the villagers of Aberafan heard the sad news that William, Duke of Normandy, had killed King Harold and seized the crown of England, it probably meant very little to them. They had their own princes, first Caradog ap Gruffydd and then Iestyn ap Gwrgant, and they had no reason to expect that what happened in far-off Sussex would ever have any importance for them. A few years later, in 1075, King William himself came riding along the old Roman road on a pilgrimage to St. Davids, but even then they had no reason to expect trouble. (Though perhaps their princes wondered why a humble pilgrim came with so many soldiers – if so, they were wise to wonder. William had his own plans for Wales.)

The Duke of Normandy had no legal right to the throne of England, and he had recruited a large army to help him conquer his new kingdom. Now he needed to find some way of keeping his most powerful followers occupied, so that they would not do to him what they had done to Harold. He decided to kill two birds with one stone: he would reward his knights with estates along the Welsh borders, and then encourage them to conquer new lands inside Wales itself, thus keeping both sets of potential enemies busy fighting each other.

We know very little about the coming of the Normans, but there is a well-known legend which tells the story of the Twelve Knights. According to this, Iestyn ap Gwrgant first seized the kingdom of Morgannwg (Glamorgan) from Caradog ap Gruffydd, and then turned to the kingdom of Deheubarth (West Wales), which was ruled by Rhys ap Tewdwr. Iestyn's cousin, Einion ap Collwyn, was in England at the time, and Iestyn used him as a go-between to persuade the Norman Knight Robert Fitzhamon, and a number of others, to join him in getting rid of Rhys. Once Rhys was dead, the Normans were paid for their help and set off back to England; but then Iestyn refused to give his cousin Einion what had been promised to

16

him (Iestyn's daughter as his wife), and Einion, furious, intercepted Fitzhamon's band and persuaded them to come back and overthrow Iestyn himself. After that the Normans stayed in Glamorgan and divided it up between themselves.

This makes a good romantic story, but there is no serious evidence that Einion ap Collwyn ever existed, and many of the details of the story (first written down by Sir Edward Stradling of St. Donats almost five hundred years later) are incorrect. However, it is quite possible that the Normans could have used some such quarrel between the Welsh princes to help them get a foothold inside Wales, and once they were in Glamorgan, they made quite sure that they stayed.

Although there is no record of any fighting near Aberafan, the villagers who lived near the ford over the river Afan must have become used to seeing parties of armed men riding backwards and forwards along the high road. Normans built castles at Neath and Swansea, and held the rich areas of Gower, as they held all the best land in the Vale; only the barren mountain country was left to the Welsh. At Aberafan the hills came very near to the sea, and so the country between the river Afan and the river Neath was duly presented to Iestyn's son Caradoc, first of the Lords of Afan. Yet although this lordship contained comparatively little fertile ground, it did have a strategic value, holding the river crossing, and it seems a little strange that the Normans allowed Caradoc and his heirs to control this – they were never collaborators, and attacked the Normans almost as often as they attacked their own Welsh kinsmen.

One of Caradoc's first actions was to build a castle. This, like most of the earliest castles, was simply an earth mound with a wooden fence marking off a courtyard (or bailey) in front of the mound. (These were known as 'motte and bailey' castles.) The castle was built next to the present site of St. Mary's church (which was founded at about the same time), and the names of Castle Street and Bailey Street still remind passers-by of where it stood.

We know that this first castle was probably built of wood because in 1153 it was attacked and burned down by Maredudd and Rhys ap Gruffydd, the grandsons of Rhys ap Tewdwr. Maredudd and Rhys were brothers-in-law to Caradoc ap Iestyn,

17

The earliest Norman Castles were built of wood. (c. 1150 A.D.)
(David West)

who had married their sister Gwladys, but Caradoc himself probably died about 1147, so it was their nephew Morgan whom the two West Walian princes were attacking. The *Chronicle of the Princes* gives a vivid picture of events:

'And the month of May following, Maredudd and Rhys, sons of Gruffydd, jointly attacked the castle of Aberafan, and after killing the garrison and burning the castle, they brought from thence immense spoil and innumerable riches.'

Almost at once Morgan ap Caradoc rebuilt the castle, this time in stone, and there are no further records of it being damaged or besieged, no doubt much to the relief of the people living round it. The chronicle only mentions the slaughter of the castle garrison, not of the townspeople, but it is doubtful whether the latter escaped totally unharmed; at the very least their homes would have been in danger of catching fire. And since it is likely that many of them were either the families of the castle garrison, or tradesmen or craftsmen who had come to serve it, they were probably in as much danger as the soldiers themselves.

The population of Aberafan at that time may have been no more than a hundred altogether. A small hamlet was likely to grow up at the lowest crossing point of any largish river, to provide for all who passed that way; since the lower reaches of the river were tidal, bad weather and high tides could hold travellers up for days, or even weeks, and they needed ferrymen and/or guides to help them across the water, as well as food and shelter while they waited. Then, when Caradoc ap Iestyn built his castle there would be a further need, first for men to build it, and then for others, to defend it; if they did not bring their families with them, then no doubt they soon began new ones in their new home.

So we can imagine the little castle sitting proudly on its mound above the courtyard; just across the moat is the small, very simple parish church, dedicated to St. Mary, and clustering round the castle gate and the church are the mud and stone houses of the little town, with a blacksmith's forge, an inn, and somewhere nearby, a mill belonging the lord of Afan, where the townspeople's corn is ground for a fee paid to the lord. The houses are small and dark, with earth floors and no fireplaces or chimneys or glass in the windows. They would have had very little furniture except for benches and stools, a chest or two for storage, trestles for the table and some sort of bed. Yet to our eyes the castle itself does not seem much more luxurious. Here too there is very little furniture, perhaps a few hangings to keep out the draughts, and rushes on the floor to act as a disposable carpet (sweep out the rushes once a week and all the rubbish goes with them). Probably Caradoc's wife Gwladys and her daughter-in-law Gwenllian have a solar, a private room to withdraw to, but otherwise the people in the castle live as much on top of one another as the townspeople in their cottages.

There is a pleasant, if rather doubtful, legend about Caradoc ap Iestyn which says that one day, when he was being chased by his enemies, he headed for Aberafan castle – only to find, when he got there, that the place was empty. In desperation Caradoc hid himself in a dark corner and waited to be discovered; but then, as his pursuers began to search the castle buildings, the castle doves flew up and began to circle overhead. When they saw this, the searchers decided that Caradoc could not be hiding there – if he had gone to the castle, the doves would have been disturbed already, before his pursuers arrived. They went away, leaving Caradoc in safety (and anxious, one suspects, to tell the captain of the garrison what he thought of his leaving the castle undefended).

Caradoc ap Iestyn was succeeded as the lord of Afan by his eldest son, Morgan. Morgan's brothers, Maredudd, Cadwallon and Owain, shared the rest of their father's lands, but Cadwallon wanted more and murdered Owain; then Cadwallon himself was killed when the wall of a castle he was attacking fell on him. What the people of Aberafan thought of their quarrelsome princes, we do not know, but they must have listened with great interest to the story of Owain's greyhound, which fought to save its master even when it had been wounded by arrows and spear thrusts. (When its wounds were healed, it was sent to King Henry II as evidence of the tale.)

This was the time, too, of the great famine. Precisely why there was a famine we do not know; perhaps the previous year's crops had been blighted by storms or disease, but in any case there was a shortage of food. People hurried to Margam Abbey (founded in 1147) and waited there for help, but eventually even the Abbey's supplies ran low, and the whole district faced the possibility of starvation. The monks sent a ship to Bristol to buy corn there, but its return was delayed by contrary winds, and many of the families in Aberafan must have gone to bed hungry while they waited for the much-needed cargo. Then, all at once – and a month early – the wheat in one of the fields near the abbey ripened overnight, and the monks and their congregation were saved.

This story and that of Owain's greyhound were first written down by Morgan ap Caradoc's second cousin, Gerald de Barri, better known as 'Gerald the Welshman'. Gerald was a famous churchman and scholar, and in 1188 he was sent to guide the Archbishop of Canterbury round Wales on a recruiting tour for the Third Crusade, starting out from Herefordshire, and heading down through Abergavenny, Newport and Cardiff. At length they reached Margam and Gerald tells a number of stories about the abbey, some of which he perhaps learned from his cousin Morgan ap Caradoc, who acted as the party's guide through the perils of the coast road and the crossing of the river Neath. No doubt Morgan would have been happy to welcome the Archbishop to Aberafan Castle, but the accommodation at Margam Abbey was more suitable for a great churchman and his retinue, and so the local people only saw the great men as they rode through the town.

Gerald's description gives some idea of the hazards of travel in the twelfth century. The coast road was nearer to the sea shore then, it seems, because Gerald speaks of 'the twin hazards of a sandy shore and an incoming tide'; this must have made heavy going for the packhorses that carried the Archbishop's luggage. There was no bridge across the Afan as yet, so when they reached the ford through the river, Gerald and the rest had to wait until the tide went out and the river was a its shallowest before they could cross. It was still only mid-March, and although Gerald does not mention it, it seems likely that Morgan would have invited the party into his castle to warm themselves and take some refreshment after all the time spent hanging about in the sharp morning air, waiting till they could ford the Afan. Perhaps one of the party was sent out to preach the crusade to the wondering townspeople; the base of a 'preaching cross' which once stood in the centre of Aberafan can still be seen outside St. Mary's Church, and perhaps some 800 years ago Archbishop Baldwin's interpreter stood beside it and urged his listeners to join the army that was to go and free Jerusalem from the infidel. Then Morgan led them along the coast-road to the river Neath, where they had further adventures with the quicksands that barred the way to the ferry (the ford was too dangerous to use).

(Other distinguished mediaeval travellers who passed through Aberafan included King John in 1210; Edward I in 1284; Edward II in 1326; and Richard II in 1394 and 1399, en route to Ireland.)

Morgan ap Caradoc was dead by 1208 by the latest, and was succeeded by his son Leisan; but Leisan too seems to have died by 1217, and the lordship of Afan went to his brother, another Morgan, who was nicknamed Morgan Gam (or 'crooked'). Morgan Gam, like his father, led a hectic life, attacking the Normans at Neath and Margam whenever possible, and even spending a year in chains in an English prison, but ultimately he came home, and when he died in 1241 he too was buried at Margam Abbey. He was followed by his eldest son, Leisan, but Leisan died without heirs, and the lordship went to the second son, another Morgan, known as Morgan Fychan (or the 'younger'). Leisan and Morgan seem to have led a quieter life than their father – no doubt much to the relief of their tenants at Aberafan, since even if most of the fighting took place elsewhere, at Margam or Neath or Kenfig, the townspeople cannot have been happy to see their husbands and sons marching off to war so often. There was no Geneva Convention in those days, and even if one survived the fighting, summary executions, blinding or branding were all possibilities for the soldiers of a defeated army.

The military conquest of Glamorgan had been quick and thorough, and though the Lords of Afan continued to fight, they were defending their own position against both the Normans and their fellow Welshmen; there was no question of trying to expel the invaders permanently. It took much longer, though, for the descendants of Caradoc ap Iestyn to accept Norman ideas, and it was not until Morgan Gam married a Norman heiress, Matilda de Braose, that they began to realise their future lay in co-operation, not conflict. Morgan's

22

daughter Matilda married a Turberville (of Coity Castle), and his son Morgan Fychan married the daughter of Walter de Sully; Morgan's son Leisan was knighted, and adopted a coat of arms in true Anglo-Norman style.

This slow change of attitude was to have long-term effects on the little community at the castle gates. No doubt the Norman wives brought new customs and new fashions in food, dress and furnishings to interest the housewives of Aberafan. Gerald of Wales tells us in his book *The Description of Wales,* that the Welsh lived chiefly on oats, milk, cheese, butter and meat, and ate little bread; there was no 'variety of dishes' or 'highly seasoned titbits', and the food was served on large plates, each holding enough for three people. On the other hand, hospitality was complete; 'everyone's home is open to all'. The traveller just walked into the nearest house, handed over his weapons, and was given water. If he washed his feet with the water, then he was asking to stay overnight; if not, he just wanted refreshments and meant to go on his way after a short rest. This freedom and hospitality, not to mention the somewhat monotonous diet, must have seemed very strange to Matilda de Braose and her daughter-in-law.

Gerald also comments that his fellow countrymen 'pay no attention to commerce, shipping or industry.' The Anglo-Normans, however, though they might not take part in trade themselves, were quick to see how they could make money from encouraging it, and this was something that Leisan ap Morgan Fychan soon adopted for his own lands, along with his coat of arms and an English-style surname – d'Avene. (He also gave his sons English names – John and Thomas.)

Just as the household in the castle had expanded and adapted new ideas, so had the town outside the castle gates. Aberafan was not a natural market town; it was not the centre of a broad fertile valley like Neath, or the meeting point of many roads or rivers like Bridgend. Cwmafan, its nearest agricultural area, was a narrow valley, with roads so bad that it was easier to get to Neath than to Aberafan. On the other hand, Aberafan did have certain useful qualities of its own. It was on the coast road through South Wales, so that everyone travelling that way, from kings and archbishops to beggars and wandering minstrels, had to go through the town, and it also had a harbour which was

23

Castles were rebuilt in stone in the Twelfth Century
(David West)

already being used by the monks of Margam to export their wool. (The monks, incidentally, had also begun to work the local coal seams, though not to export coal commercially – the workings were still on a very small scale.)

Then, somewhere around 1304, Sir Leisan d'Avene issued a charter, the first official record of the borough of Aberafan. Whether this was Leisan's own idea, to encourage trade and earn himself a few useful fees, or whether the townspeople approached him and asked for a charter, we do not know, but almost certainly Leisan's charter was the first to be granted to the town, because otherwise he would have quoted from earlier grants (as his grandson Thomas quoted from Leisan's when he reissued the charter in 1350).

In his charter Leisan begins by stating that he and his heirs grant to all his 'English burgesses and chancers (market traders) of Avene' the same liberties as the burgesses of Kenfig enjoy. Then he goes on to say that the burgesses are to give eight jars from every brewing in payment for their use of his mill, while he will allow them to take timber for fires and hedges from his woods, and pasture their animals anywhere on his lands once the crops have been harvested – or on top of Mynydd Dinas at any time. (The right of common pasture also applies to the lands of his tenants.) However, if any of the cattle belonging to the burgesses and chancers should break into any areas enclosed by Leisan or his heirs, then the owners of the cattle will be obliged to make good the damage. In return for all these concessions the burgesses and chancers have paid Leisan forty shillings sterling. (Probably equivalent to several hundred pounds today.)

At first sight this seems to have little or nothing to do with setting up a thriving commercial community, but the important point for the burgesses was the reference to the liberties of Kenfig. The first charter of Kenfig still on record is that granted by Thomas le Despenser in 1397, but any earlier charters were probably similar enough for us to use the 1397 charter as a model. First and foremost, the burgesses there were allowed to set up a guild, to regulate trade; no strangers were allowed to sell their goods in the town, and all shopkeepers, innkeepers and brewers, even those who actually lived in Kenfig (or Aberafan), had to belong to the guild before they could carry on their business. Furthermore, all the merchants were encouraged to live and trade only in the town itself, and not go off to the 'uplands' (the hill country) to look for business – presumably so that all potential customers would have to come down to Aberafan and pay the tolls due on any goods they bought there. Tolls were also payable on any animals or goods passing through the town; the constable had the right to inspect these.

In return for observing these limitations, the individual burgesses were allowed certain advantages: freedom from paying charges for any public works, the right to bail for most offences, and freedom from the duty 'to watch fugitives in the church'. (St. Mary's church would have provided sanctuary for fugitives, whether criminals or political offenders, but the fugitive was not allowed to leave the church limits, and guards were usually set to see that the 'sanctuary men' did not escape.)

The charter also gave the burgesses the right to hold two fairs annually, probably on the dates listed in another charter of 1373; these were the feasts of St. John the Baptist (June 24th) and All Saints (November 1st). In addition to this, a number of officials were appointed, including a portreeve (or mayor), a constable of the castle, a recorder, a common attorney (for legal matters), four haywards, a pound keeper, and two ale tasters. It is an odd mixture of civic officials, trading standards officers, and enforcers of agricultural harmony. Clearly the burgesses were almost as much farmers as traders.

It is interesting to see that Leisan speaks of his 'English burgesses'. Towns were not a Welsh institution, and quite probably the Lord of Afan sent to England – perhaps to Bristol – to find experienced merchants willing to set up a trading community in Aberafan. Leisan himself would have taken a share of the tolls collected at the markets, and he would have had the benefit of a variety of shops and craftsmen at his own front door. (In this Aberafan may well have been a trend-setter – the very first Welsh authority to encourage foreign investment.)

Even now the town probably had only a hundred or so inhabitants. On market days customers would crowd in, and the officially registered traders would set up stalls, as they do today – these were the 'chancers' mentioned in the charter – but

FORTNAM'S
Specialists in Ladies and Children's Wear

— COSTUMIERS —

Costumes
and Coats
made to
Measure.

Personal
Attention,
Reliable
Service and
Highest
Quality at
Keenest
Competitive
Prices.

Hosiery a
Special
Feature.

Ici on Parle Français.

5a and 6, STATION ROAD,
PORT TALBOT.

In 1910 this was W. Newark Lewis's 'Hogarth Art Studios', specialising in 'highclass and artistic photography'. It is now part of Court's Furnishers, but in 1922 Messrs Fortnam clearly hoped for international custom.

then they would move on to the next town, leaving Aberafan in peace. In the meantime the burgesses and their families lived a life that was half that of farmers, pasturing their cattle on the common lands, and half that of craftsmen or merchants, building up their stock, ready for the next market or fair. As for the young men of Afan, they had a number of opportunities to travel, following their lord on campaigns in Scotland and France as well as locally, and returning home with both plunder and new ideas; Aberafan might be small but it was in no way isolated from modern developments.

Sir Leisan was first succeeded by his son, Sir John, and then by his grandson Thomas, who issued a new charter in 1350; the burgesses paid him two silver marks for this. What happened next is not clear. The last mention of Thomas is on February the 12th, 1359; by 1373, only fourteen years later, the lordship had passed to Edward le Despenser, Lord of Glamorgan, who issued yet another charter for the borough of Aberafan. According to some genealogies, Thomas married Maud Blount and had two sons, Thomas the younger and Morgan; another source states that Thomas's daughter Jane married Sir William Blount and exchanged the lordship of Afan for some Despenser lands in England. The truth of this cannot now be determined, but we do know that one Leisan d'Avene was involved in land transactions with Despenser in 1375-6, and it seems likely that he was Thomas's son and/or heir. Leisan went off to Lincolnshire to become a collector of taxes, and after almost three hundred years the senior branch of the lords of Afan disappeared from history, leaving only the ghostly 'White Lady' of Aberafan castle as their memorial.

The change of ownership did make some difference to the people of Aberafan because of the situation recorded in the new charter. This was purely commercial, dealing with tolls and duties on trade and goods, with no clauses about pasture rights or gathering firewood (which were probably taken for granted by now). It is just possible to see from the terms of the charter how the change of 'owner' had also changed the position of the town officials and given them more in-dependence. Despenser was a great nobleman who spent most of his time at Court; in Wales his headquarters were at Cardiff, and the charter appoints the Portreeve of Aberafan to the task not only of collecting any tolls, but also of accounting for them at Cardiff. Whether anyone now lived in Aberafan castle we do not know; perhaps it became an official residence for the Constable of the Castle, but in any case the burgesses no longer had a resident landlord to keep an eye on them.

Chapter 3

Floods and Felons

When the last of the Lords of Afan left for England, they left behind them a small, relatively obscure town, with no very obvious resources; the mineral wealth in the hills behind was largely untouched at that point. However Aberafan already had its two greatest assets – its geographical position on the main east-west road through South Wales, and its access to the sea. At that time the river Afan did not run straight into the sea as it does now; it swung round to the south east, to join the Ffrwdwyllt at a natural harbour known as the Bar of Afan. The harbour had already been used by the monks of Margam Abbey who exported their wool from it (and imported necessary supplies such as the corn from Bristol that Gerald of Wales mentioned), and once the industrial development of Aberafan began, the harbour was to come into its own.

That, however, was still several centuries away in 1485 when Ieuan Lloyd Vaughan was appointed Constable of the castles of Neath and Aberafan – only to be succeeded by John Tremaylle in the following year. Neither of these men were great lords, and their presence (assuming that the post was not simply a sinecure, perhaps a reward for supporting the new King, Henry VII, during the Bosworth campaign), was un-likely to hinder the burgesses of Aberafan in their daily ativities. As for the burgesses themselves, they already had a strong sense of civic dignity, and the Aberafan borough mace, which apparently dates back to the late fifteenth century, is the only Welsh mace surviving from that date. It was carried in front of the Portreeve (or mayor) and the other borough officials whenever they walked in procession: on feast days, for instance, or when they were proclaiming the boundaries of the borough.

(It is possible, by the way, that Aberafan was once a walled town. A borough ordinance, dated 1643, mentions the 'town walls', but since there is neither physical evidence nor any ancient tradition of such a thing, perhaps the ordinance was merely referring to the boundaries of the town, marked by a ditch or hedge. On the other hand, if Aberafan *was* walled, it might help to explain why the earlier lords of Afan were apparently able to go raiding their neighbours without suffering any serious reprisals. Perhaps their stronghold was too well defended to make such reprisals worthwhile.)

One long-standing problem with which the burgesses had to deal was that of flooding. Both the lords of Afan and the monks of Margam were always much concerned with the upkeep of the sea defences on the marshes, and it was something on which they were always willing to co-operate. However even the best defences were not always enough, and in 1427 the whole of the Swansea Bay area suffered from heavy flooding; in that year 'It rained almost continually from Easter to Michaelmas, and the hay and corn harvests were greatly hindered'. There was severe flooding again in 1491-2, at Aberafan itself.

Perhaps it was the aftermath of some such flooding that caused John Leland to comment so disparagingly on the area when he passed through Aberafan in 1540. (Leland had been appointed to the post of 'King's Antiquary' by Henry VIII, and it was his job to travel round England and Wales gathering information on the country and recording it for the king's benefit.) He began well by commenting that there was excellent woodland around Aberafan, but then he went on to add: 'There is a poor village on the west bank of the Afan, about two miles from the mouth of the river. This village is called Aberafan. The ground about it is barren and sour. This village lies in the great highway through Glamorganshire. There is a haven for ships at the mouth of this Afan . . . From the mouth of the Afan to the mouth of the river Neath is about 2 miles and a half, along a low shore choked with Severn sands and some marshy ground'. (Extract slightly modernised.)

A little further on Leland speaks of the bridges over the Afan, and curiously does not mention one in the town itself, only those higher up the river; presumably there *was* one by now, but it is just possible that this had been swept away by a sea flood which had also soured the land. (The marshes were not remarkable for their fertility, but they did produce adequate crops in normal seasons; they were below sea level, so that keeping the sea walls and the sand dunes in good repair was vital.)

31

As it happens, we know the names of many of the towns-people who watched Leland ride through Aberafan. Some two years or so after his visit, a tax was raised and the list of the names of the thirty householders who contributed, together with the amounts they paid, still survives. The seemingly dry figures give a fascinating glimpse of the social hierarchy of the little town. Twenty-two of the householders paid less than ten pence; four, including David ap Hopkyn who was the tax collector for the district, paid twenty pence; and another four, clearly the town's plutocracy, paid more than twenty pence. (Hywel ap Ieuan Mawr must have been in the millionaire class, since he paid six shillings and eight pence – eighty pence, more than twice the amount due from his nearest rival, Thomas David.) David ap Hopkyn got some compensation for what was probably a thoroughly unpopular task since he was allowed a fee of two pence for his labours. The town contributed twenty nine shillings and four pence altogether, the equivalent of several hundred pounds today.

Two points about the list are particularly interesting. Firstly, all the names are Welsh, so that in the two hundred years or so since Leisan d'Avene's original charter, all his famous English burgesses had either been driven out or (more likely) absorbed; and secondly, though Welsh surnames were still not completely fixed at that point, and often still lacked the typical 's', the thirty surnames listed are almost all still familiar in the town – Hopkin, Jenkin, David, Richard, Lewis, Llywellyn, etc. There is incidentally, one woman included – Kathryn Gryffyth, who paid two pence; she was probably the widow of one of the burgesses, whose rights in the town property she would have inherited 'for the term of her natural life' (unless she remarried).

If we allow an average of four to a household, then the population of Aberafan was by now about 120 men, women and children. The castle was probably already falling into ruin; the constables who were appointed during the sixteenth century were usually nobleman of high standing, like Sir Mathew Cradock or Henry, Earl of Worcester, who would pocket any fees due from the post, but had no intention of exercising any authority in the town, let alone living there. (In 1590 the constable was George Williams of Blaen Baglan, a descendent of the lords of Afan; but he was a local man with a fine new house of his own.) It is likely that some of the local inns dated from this period. While Margam Abbey was still flourishing, most travellers would have stopped there and enjoyed its free hospitality, but by 1540 the monks had been expelled and Leland and others like him would have been looking for lodgings in Aberafan; inns like the Angel, the Bear, the Ship, the Globe or the Red Lion may well have been set up in the sixteenth century to meet this demand. (The Lamb and Flag, another of the town inns demolished in the nineteen seventies, took its name from the badge of the lords of Afan.)

Another of the roles fulfilled by the monasteries was that of looking after the sick and the poor, like a combination of the NHS and DSS. When the monasteries were closed down and the buildings sold to county families (as Margam Abbey was sold to the Mansels) all those who had been receiving help from the monks were driven out and left to roam the country-side. Many were forced to turn to petty crime to feed themselves and their families, and the Poor Law often treated them quite savagely. Every town would have its lockup and its stocks, and persistent offenders might be flogged through the streets, branded, or even hanged, for what would seem to us quite trivial offences. All these were public spectacles, and Aberafan must have had its share of them. In earlier centuries the lords of Afan had their own court with powers of life and death (there was a field on Mynydd Dinas known as Cae'r Grogwydd, or Gallows field), and the burgesses of Aberafan inherited this court and dealt with local evildoers in it, as well as with the beggars and discharged soldiers who wandered the high roads and caused terror in the hearts of sober, respectable citizens. (Our ancestors were not nearly as settled as we sometimes believe; for instance, one Rice Lougher, very possibly a local man, was hanged at Romford in Essex in 1574, 'for stealing soldiers' money'.)

In January 1607 the burgesses had something more immediate to worry about, when the Swansea Bay area was hit by a tidal wave. Many were drowned, both people and animals, and corn, hay and other provisions were spoiled and lost (presumably when the barns they were stored in were washed

**In 1909, long
before the N.H.S.
arrived, there were
more colourful
methods of funding
health care!**

**Even in 1922 local
chemists were expected
to include agricultural
supplies such as sheep
dips in their stock.**

away). This could have been worse, since at least the survivors could look forward to gathering new crops in a few months' time, but there must have been many nights when they went to bed hungry in that Spring of 1607. As far as Aberafan was concerned, the first priority was to repair the sea walls and the drainage systems on the marshes, and these repairs proved so costly that the people of the town appealed to the Portreeve and officials of Swansea for financial aid; they were given a grant of twenty shillings (one pound). However the sea and river defences contrived to need careful attention for many years after that; in 1659 the bailiff of Evan Seys, Sergeant at Law, asked for permission from the Mansels to gather stones in the river Afan 'to repair a breach in his land'.

Whatever the possible danger from tidal waves or marauding vagrants, life must still have been comparatively peaceful for the inhabitants of Aberafan in the early seventeenth century. A set of ordinances (or regulations) for the running of the borough's affairs has survived from the year 1643, and it deals with such matters as how to become a burgess, the fines to be levied on non-burgesses trying to trade in the town, or on burgesses failing to carry out their civic duties. The eight clauses end with two dealing with the appointment of an official pound keeper, and with the penalties for keeping sheep or goats within the town walls. Clearly the burgesses were still as much farmers as traders. (The list of those liable to pay the Ship Money tax in 1634 includes three freeholders from the borough: Griffith ap Ieuan, Jenkin William and Henry Prees. These were probably farmers whose lands came within the borough limits.)

Yet in 1643, while the burgesses were busy regulating trade and organising goats, England was already in chaos from the civil war between King Charles I and the Parliamentarians. Slowly the war spread into Wales, and a number of the Welsh castles were besieged by the Parliamentary forces – mostly in South-East and North Wales. However the First Civil War (1642-47) had little effect locally. Then in 1648 war broke out again in various places, including Wales, and a number of the rebels took refuge in Pembroke Castle. Oliver Cromwell decided that he would deal with this particular threat in person, and travelled along the main coast road through South Wales at the head of his army.

35

When Cromwell got to Aberafan, or so the story goes, he found that the town's inhabitants were staunch Royalists, and he decided to punish them by taking away their charter. According to one version, he set up his temporary quarters at the Ship Inn and sent a detachment of troopers to collect the document which was in the charge of the current Portreeve., However this gentleman (perhaps Matthew James, Portreeve in 1643) had prior notice of the coming of the soldiers; he was chopping wood at the time, and slipped the charter inside a hollow in his chopping block. The Roundheads questioned the Portreeve sternly, but he denied all knowledge of the vital document, and though they searched everywhere, they could not find it.

Luckily for the townspeople, Cromwell decided that his appointment in Pembroke was more important than finding the charter, and he left without pursuing the matter further. As they watched his army march off to the west, the inhabitants of Aberafan (and the Portreeve in particular) must have been giving the heartiest of thanks to whatever power had preserved them. Neither Cromwell nor the Parliamentarians were noted for being merciful. (The chopping block has been preserved, and can still be seen at the Civic Centre – almost on the very spot where it played its part in saving the day for Aberafan).

The importance of the charter was that it was the townspeople's only proof of the rights and the independence they claimed. Without the actual document, anyone could step in and trade in the town, or refuse to pay tolls, and the burgesses would have no legal way of stopping them. They *could* ask whoever was in power to grant a new charter confirming their ancient rights – but they would have to pay for that, and the authorities could ask for whatever sum they chose as payment; more, perhaps, than the burgesses could afford without beggaring themselves.

We do not know whether the townspeople were staunchly Royalist, as the story suggests. Most of the Mansel family supported the King (apart from Bussy Mansel of Briton Ferry who was the commander of the local Parliamentary forces), but the townspeople do not seem to have been as much under the control of the local gentry as other towns often were.

However, the vicar of St. Mary's Church was removed from his living in 1650 because he refused to comply with the new forms of worship ordained by Parliament, which might suggest some Royalist/Anglican sympathies in the town. This vicar was a Mr. David; he was replaced by David Walters, an itinerant preacher with Baptist leanings, but in 1660, when the king came back and the Anglican services were restored, Vicar David also returned to his living and it was Mr. Walters's turn to pack his bags.

Up until this point the people of Aberafan seem to have been thoroughly orthodox in religion, following the practices of the established church whichever it was, first Roman Catholic and then Anglican. Now, however, we begin to hear of the town's first nonconformists, a small group of Baptists – encouraged, perhaps, by the arrival of David Walters. There were seven known members in Aberafan: Robert Hopkin, John Williams, John Bevan, David Hopkin, Judith Thomas, Gwenllian Henry and Elinor Watkin. They did not have a chapel, but met in each other's houses for worship, on Sundays and Thursdays, and came under the local leadership of Robert Thomas of Baglan Hall (a descendent of the lords of Afan).

No doubt the ordinary people of the town were delighted when Cromwell gave way to Charles II, and the repressive rule of the Puritans was ended. Once again they could celebrate Christmas, and attend the candle-lit service before dawn known as the Plygain; once again they could play games in the churchyard after Service on Sunday and celebrate feasts like that of St. John's Eve, June 24th, with its fair, and bonfires and merrymaking in the evening. There were old customs too, like the Mari Lwyd at Christmas and Calennig at New Year, and every inn would have had its harpist to entertain travellers. Life was hard in those days, with natural disasters like flooding, and epidemics like the Great Plague of 1665, which claimed its victims in Wales just as cruelly as in devastated London, but there were compensations too, and our ancestors knew very well how to enjoy them.

Chapter 4

Forging Ahead

Round about the year 1695 Edward Lhuyd, the keeper of the Ashmolean Museum in Oxford, decided to write a book on the history and antiquities of Wales. He contacted friends and acquaintances all over Wales – usually the vicar or the squire of each place – and asked them to send him an account of their own parish; the book was never written, but many of the parish descriptions still survive, including those for the Afan District.

The Baglan account, which was written by Anthony Thomas of Baglan Hall, is full of curious details about local coal mining; the description of Aberafan is not so full, but is still of considerable interest. The writer mentions the old tradition of the first town lost under the 'Sea and Sands', and the 'Ruinous Castle, by whome founded I know not', as well as the two ruined crosses, one (the base of which still exists) in St. Mary's churchyard, and one in the centre of the town. By now, it seems, the lands once owned by the Lords of Afan had become the property of the borough corporation, and the writer goes on to describe how the burgesses shared up their meadows. The account is not altogether clear (and does not agree with later reports), but basically the suggestion is that some of the land was enclosed, and this was shared between the three Senior Burgesses; these three also had shares in the unenclosed common land, which was otherwise divided between the Junior Burgesses. Each burgess held his land for life plus six years; if he was married, his widow held it for her lifetime plus six years, unless she remarried, and either the burgess or his widow could choose to whom the land would go after their deaths. At this point, of course, while the town's population was still very small (about 180 people), almost every adult male must have been a burgess, so that there were unlikely to be any problems over land ownership; but that would change once Aberafan began to grow.

It seems that the common lands of the borough fell into two parts – 'Aberafan Brwyn' on the moors, known as the

'Englishry', and another, on 'Mynydd Dinas' known as the 'Welshry'; the old division between the Anglo-Norman 'bro' (or vale) and the Welsh 'blaenau' (or hill country) was still remembered, even in a lordship which had been a Welsh foundation. There is also an echo of Cromwell's visit; he may not have been the only outsider to try and steal the borough charter. 'Aberafan Burgesses, notwithstanding the inveiglements of some and threats of other people, did not in the late Reigns surrender their charter – not even under the threat of legal action during the reign of James II.'

Aberafan in 1700 was still very much a farming community; the writer speaks of pasture and corn ground, of its peaty soil and the 'indifferent' fertility of the land, of the animals kept (cattle, horses, sheep, goats and pigs). The nearest approach to any sort of industry is 'some quarries of stone for building'. Strangely there is no mention at all of sea trade or the harbour, though under Baglan Anthony Thomas mentions the local fishing and comments that the people speak Welsh fluently still, despite the ancient coal trade with England. However he does comment on one industry common to both Baglan and Aberafan, which was the export of sea holly or eringoes to London (where this local product was highly regarded. Candied eringoes was a popular dish, used apparently as an aphrodisiac.)

Whether it was the quiet life or the strong sea breezes (or even the sea holly!) that was responsible, Aberafan was certainly a healthy spot in which to live, and one whose inhabitants could expect a long and vigorous life. At the time when the account was written there were several eighty-year-olds alive, and in recent memory there had been at least two who only just missed their hundredth birthday.

So far the story of Aberafan has had to be pieced together from a variety of sources, none of them giving more than a glimpse of the little community on the west bank of the river Afan. (The town had not yet spread across the river, though there were two farms on the east bank whose tenants, though technically based in Margam parish, seem to have seen themselves as belonging to Aberafan, and were buried in St. Mary's churchyard. Cwrt Ucha, on the site of the new Magistrates' Court, was one of these.)

However by the eighteenth century we begin to find a number of documentary records which give us a much fuller idea of life in the town. Firstly there were the records of the manorial courts, dating orginally from the Middle Ages, which dealt with the administration of justice – though this included a number of problems which we would not think of now as legal matters. There are the kind of cases that we would expect to find in court proceedings; in May 1707, for instance, there had been a fight between James ap John and William John, in which William John had his head broken, and in 1756 Christopher Turberville was accused of committing highway robbery in Baglan. October 1701 had seen a different sort of robbery when William Henry, Daniel Jenkin and Margaret William (all innkeepers) were accused of giving short measure (the local innkeepers were always in trouble for this kind of offence, and even a dignitary like Evan Jones, portreeve, parish clerk and landlord of the Red Lion, was liable to be accused). But time after time the court was expected to deal with civil crimes like neglecting to repair the sea walls, or failing to keep their hedges tidy; in May 1750 'Mary Pullard spinster' was fined six shillings and eight pence (34p) for not keeping her hedge in good repair, and if she failed to see to this within a fortnight, she would be liable for a further thirteen shillings and four pence. (Fines were still being assessed in terms of the mediaeval mark, also thirteen shillings and four pence.)

Sanitation was primitive in those days, and another matter of great concern to the courts was that of dunghills. Not only household rubbish, but also manure was left lying in heaps on the roadway, and in May 1753 John Lotwick and William Hadock were accused of 'laying dunghills on the Kings Rode', and fined one shilling. The dunghills were to be removed in a week under pain of a further fine of one shilling and eight pence. Four years later, twenty one people were accused of the same nuisance, and given a month to remove their rubbish. And Aberafan Bridge was definitely in existence by now, because it too was a subject of concern; in October 1750 its north pillar was in danger of collapse, and it was rebuilt in the months following.

The courts also dealt with inquests and with the disposal of wrecks and anything of interest washed up on the shore. In

October 1705 they were concerned with a cargo of copper ore (worth five shillings), which was duly assigned to the lord of the manor (the Dowager Duchess of Pembroke), and in December 1707 there was a serious argument over an unmanned barque driven ashore at Aberafan, when John David, foreman of the jury, tried to intimidate his fellow jurors. Most of the penalties seem to have been financial, but the town did have its own stocks for the punishment of minor offences, and there was a town gaol where serious criminals could be held. (The gaoler's fee was the use of half an acre of land.)

The court records are not the only source of information about life in Aberafan. The parish church naturally kept records of births, deaths and marriages, and of repairs to the church building, but the parish was also the unit of administration for the Poor Law and for the highways; the body which dealt with these was known as the 'Parish Vestry', and its meetings would be attended by the vicar, the parish clerk, the two church wardens, the overseers of the Poor Law and any of the people of the parish who wished to be present. Meetings were originally held in the church (hence the name of 'vestry'), but later they were often held in a convenient inn, and ale featured prominently in the vestry accounts, both as refreshments and as fees for services like hanging a new bell, or digging graves.

The vestry records are a curious mixture. At that time each parish was responsible for providing help for all those in need – but its responsibility was limited to those who had a 'right of settlement' in that particular parish; if anyone became a pauper and/or was taken ill and could not establish their right of settlement, they and their family would be removed as soon as possible, back to the parish where they *did* have such a right. Hence the records are full of reports of families being sent back to other parishes, and of payments being made to the overseer who went with them to make sure they got there. As to the fortunate souls who got to stay in Aberafan, the charity they received had its price, and by 1801 the 'paupers' were even obliged to wear badges to show their status. On the other hand, workhouses were not yet the order of the day, and the vestry was comparatively generous in what it provided. For instance, in 1788 it paid for two shirts, a pair of breeches and a waistcoat

41

of cloth, a waistcoat of flannel, shoes, stockings and a hat for one young lad, as well as paying the fees due when the boy's brother was bound as a parish apprentice (perhaps to a local craftsman or farmer). It paid too for paupers' funerals and medical expenses, and was always concerned to establish the paternity of illegitimate children – not for moral reasons but in order to make sure that the father took financial responsibility for his offspring.

As time went on, and the population grew, this system of 'parish relief' began to be too heavy a burden for small communities, and a harsher note enters the records. We have already seen that in 1801 the paupers were being ordered to wear badges; and a little earlier, in 1788, the vestry resolved that houses were only to be let to parishioners, and strangers would be considered only if they could produce a certificate from their original parish – that is, if the people of Aberafan could be sure that the newcomers would not become a charge on them, if they ran into trouble.

On a more rural note, one regular charge on the rates was payment for the killing of vermin, mostly foxes and owls, though there are also references to 'ffwlbarts' (polecats); the rates of payment varied considerably, from one to five shillings for a fox, and one shilling for an owl. Nowadays we would look askance at anyone killing owls or polecats – even the foxes who are sometimes seen lurking on the rough ground under the motorway would be more likely to be welcomed than killed. But our ancestors could not afford to give their wild neighbours a free hand with their crops; there was no convenient shopping centre to visit if the weather or animal predators damaged the harvest. Some idea of just how precarious life still was for them can be gathered from the story of the Great Flood of 1768, only just over two hundred years ago.

It was July 25th when the Afan flooded. According to one eye-witness 'the water flowed into St. Mary's Church and every house in Town to the height of five feet in most places, so that many persons were in the utmost danger of their lives'. Luckily most of the population escaped to higher ground, but two people, Catherine Richard and a young boy called William Bowen, were drowned; they were later buried in the same grave.

remarked that he hoped that the Admiral would remember him, the visitor burst out laughing and declared, 'I never shall forget you to the last day of my life!' (On the whole one feels that it was the Portreeve who came away from the encounter with the greater credit.)

By 1801 the population of Aberafan had risen to 275, but the place could still quite fairly be described as a 'village'. This, however was about to change, starting when S.F. Lettsom began to manufacture tinplates at the Aberafan Forge, perhaps as early as 1803. Unfortunately Lettsom had financial problems, and by 1815 the works were closed. Lettsom's troubles multiplied, but though he finally abandoned his various schemes in 1820, there were others who could also see the industrial potential in the area, and by 1822 the Aberafan Forge was in the hands of new owners, Robert Smith and John Reynolds. These men extended the Forge and set themselves up as the Margam Tinplate Works. They began with the original, or 'lower' Forge, on the site of the D.S.S. office, and then built on a site a little further up the river, at what later became the Andrew Scott Rutherglen Depot; this became known as the 'Upper Forge'.

The two men had previously managed the Carmarthen Tinplate Works, and they realised from the first that they would need experienced tinplate workers for the new venture; hence they brought many of their former employees with them. These were housed in Carmarthen Row (now demolished, but near the present Day Centre under the motorway). Technically both the Forge and the houses built for its workers were in Margam parish, not Aberafan, and so this new development is not fully reflected in the population figures, but it marks the beginning of what was to become 'Port Talbot' (as against the narrower boundaries of the ancient borough of Aberafan). Donovan's 'poor little village' was about to be transformed.

Chapter 5

Tinplate and Teachers

John Reynolds soon severed his connection with the Margam Tinplate Works and went off to Pontrhydyfen, where he was responsible for the building of the Aqueduct. Robert Smith stayed in Aberafan; he was a very unusual ironmaster, since he was a Welsh-speaking Nonconformist and something of a pioneer in the interest he took in the welfare of those who worked for him.

Nonconformity came to Aberafan in the mid-seventeenth century, when the Baptists set up a cause here, and the local Independents (Congregationalists) date from the same period. At first their meetings were illegal (though they were never persecuted as seriously as the Roman Catholics); but later the various Acts banning them were repealed and they were able to meet more freely, often in each other's houses. (The Baptists met in 'Capel Jinni', the house of a widow called Jennet, just off High Street.) For most people, however, religion was not a burning issue; they went to church on Sunday because they always had, and enjoyed the celebrations when there was a festival like Christmas or St. John's Eve, but that was all. They must have been somewhat bemused and not too favourably impressed at first when the itinerant preachers who spread the news of the Methodist Revival began to visit Aberafan in the seventeen forties. John Wesley himself visited the area on a number of occasions, though he needed an interpreter when he preached, and was not always too fortunate with the weather; but the most frequent visitor seems to have been Howel Harris.

Harris's visits were not always welcome. On one occasion when he was preaching at Aberafan a gang of young louts tried to break up the meeting by throwing a cat into the congregation and then setting a dog after it, but the meeting continued despite this. At another time he was preaching outside the Plough Inn (just across the river, more or less where the Post Office is now), when he found he needed to be raised a little higher to be heard. The landlady lent him a stool, but her husband, less friendly, grabbed it back, and there was a ding-dong struggle between husband and wife until at last the landlord gave up. Perhaps he was ultimately converted too, because a Sunday School was later held at the Plough Inn, between 1806 and 1810; it was run by one Miles Edwards.

Sunday Schools like this were a very important part of the Methodist movement. There were few, if any, schools for ordinary people in the early eighteenth century apart from the circulating schools organised by Griffith Jones of Llanddowror. These were free and offered tuition in reading in the Welsh language so that their pupils could read the Catechism and the Bible, but the teachers only stayed in one place for some three months before moving on. A number of these schools were held locally, but the movement came to an end in 1779; luckily by then the Methodists were able to take up the work and establish permanent Sunday Schools, whose emphasis was as much educational as religious. (There were also sometimes small schools run by ladies who wished to make use of their education to earn a living, like those run by Mrs. Edwards and Mrs. Reid mentioned in the government enquiry of 1847, but these would have been for the wealthier families in the community.)

At first all the local Methodists met for services at Dyffryn Barn in Margam, but in 1810 it was decided that they needed more than one meeting place, so Carmel Chapel was built. It was the first Nonconformist place of worship to be specially built in this area, and it had seating space for 200 people; it was soon followed by Capel Moriah (Baptist, 1821) and Tabernacl (Independent, 1824). The men who helped to build and run these chapels seem to have been mostly craftsmen of one sort or another – carpenters, weavers, overseers in the mines or tinplate works – at least these were the kind of men who became deacons, but naturally the congregations would tend to choose those who had already shown themselves to be competent outside the chapel. Robert Smith, of the Margam Tinplate Works, became first a member and then a deacon in Carmel, and in the Big Seat he sat alongside his own workmen. (He was unusual in his deep interest in the welfare of his workers, helping them to set up an early form of co-operative shop, and in 1833 he founded a 'works school' where both the children and the adults attached to the Tinplate Works could learn to read and study the Bible.)

The Margam Tinplate Works had a considerable effect on Aberafan. It brought new people and ideas to the town, and the rise in population associated with it meant prosperity for the local shopkeepers and professional men. In the years between 1801 and 1821 the population rose by less than 100 souls; then, in the 1831 census one can see a reflection of the new development round the tinplate works as the figures rise by 208 to a total of 573 inhabitants. By the 1841 census the population had more than doubled, to 1,290.

Yet this sudden growth was not solely due to events in Aberafan itself. The copperworks at Taibach had continued to expand, and there were coal mines in the Afan valley and at Bryn; Cwmafan was now the home of a flourishing iron, tinplate and chemical works, and its proprietors were planning to set up a copper works as well. All of this meant that the old harbour at the Bar of Afan was no longer adequate for the cargoes that needed to be shipped in and out of the area, and in 1834 the English Copper Co. (of Taibach), John Vigurs and Thomas Reynolds (of the Cwmafan Works) and C.R.M. Talbot of Margam Castle got together to form a new company to build a floating dock.

No doubt the industrialists enrolled C.R.M. Talbot in their company in order to make certain that the two Acts of Parliament necessary to allow them to build the dock would pass into law, but Talbot exacted his price in more than financial terms. The second act, of 1836, which allowed them to divert the river Afan directly into the sea, also stated that the new harbour was to be known as Port Talbot. The first ship sailed into the new dock on March 18th, 1837 (though work on the harbour continued for another four years.)

In 1831, some three years before work began on the harbour, Aberafan saw a rather less happy event. Among the worshippers at the newly built Carmel Chapel had been Lewis and Mary Lewis, a sober, Godfearing couple whose young son Richard had learnt to read in the Sunday School connected with the chapel. In 1819, when the boy was eleven years old, the family moved to Merthyr Tydfil, and in 1831 Richard, now better known by his nickname of Dic Penderyn, was found guilty of stabbing a soldier during the Merthyr Rising. He was sentenced to death, and duly hanged at Cardiff Gaol on August 13th, 1831; his body was brought back to Aberafan on a cart and buried in St. Mary's churchyard on the next day, August 14th. A vast crowd accompanied the funeral party, and the service had to be held out in the churchyard; Dic's brother-in-law, the Methodist preacher Morgan Howells, gave the address.

It is a sad story, but it throws some light on the town itself and its independence. Dic had been wrongly convicted, as an example to all those who dared to stand against the ironmasters and their friends, but Aberafan allowed him to have a funeral that was almost a public triumph, and his memory was honoured locally during the years when Merthyr itself had temporarily forgotten him. (Dic's was not the only cause to be upheld by the community at Aberafan; twenty years later, when the Nonconformists in Cwmafan were being persecuted by the manager of the Works there, Aberafan supported them and allowed them to hold meetings in the town.)

Five years later, in 1836, a group of visitors from Oxford came to stay at Brombil House; they were friends of Robert Smith and his family, and one of them, Esther Phillips Williams, kept a diary of her visit. On Saturday, July 22nd the party went to see the Margam Tin Works, visiting the Lower Forge, and Esther noted that though some of the workers were clearly suffering from the dirt and heat in which they worked, the rest, men, women and children, 'appeared clean as well as contented and happy'. She also noticed that there was an oven next to the coke furnaces, 'where the poor women came every Saturday to bake their bread'. (It was not only the poor who profited from this; even in the earlier part of this century it was quite usual for housewives to get part of their cooking done at the local baker's or a similar 'public' oven.) On the Sunday the visitors went to inspect the Works' School, which was large enough to accommodate two to three hundred people. Mr. Smith led the congregation in Welsh hymn-singing, and his guests were happy to see that the singers were all, even those 'so squalid and dirty' the day before, 'a pattern of neatness and cleanliness'.

Evidently the visitors from Oxford were fascinated by the power and majesty of the machinery in the tinplate works, but

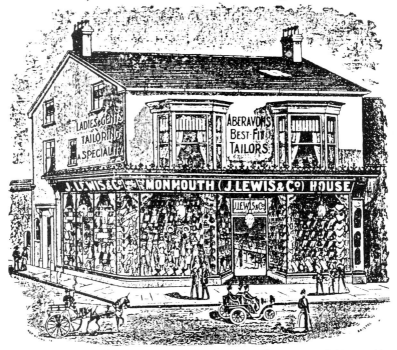

they did not spend all their time there and the diary gives what may be the first ever description of a trip to Aberafan Beach. 'The sands here are extensive and firm . . . Behind us were nothing but hills of sand, and before us was the wide spreading sea. We enjoyed a ride for two or three miles . . .'

The diary mentions in passing that the workers included men, women and children, and this was not unusual at that time. Women always worked in the tinplate works, of course, even after they were banned from working underground in the mines, but in those days most children also worked, in one way or another; only the aristocracy and middle classes automatically sent their sons and daughters to school. The children might help on the farm, or in the workshop, or wherever the family workplace might be; their labour and the money they earned were essential to the family budget. When possible they would be sent to school for a year or two (as Dic Penderyn was), but the father who carried his tiny child down the mine with him was only following an old tradition. Not everyone was prepared to accept this, and in 1842 a Royal Commission enquired into the conditions under which children worked in the mines and elsewhere. Probably few of the Aberafan children worked in the mines, but the tinplate works was equally dangerous, with the risk of injury from unguarded machinery or hot metal, and all those employed would have worked anything up to fourteen hours a day or more. The vicar of Aberafan, when questioned by the enquiry, said that the local children had become 'so weary that they were indifferent about attending school'; they started work when they were about eight years of age. The growth of those working in the tinworks was stunted, and the girls tended to suffer from chlorosis (or green sickness – a kind of anaemia).

Despite this, it does seem that the various local employers did at least intend to treat their child workers reasonably well, and set minimum ages for employment 'unless at the express wish of the parents'. However, an act was passed, and women, girls and boys under ten were no longer allowed to work underground; other acts controlled the employment of children in factories and cut the long working day.

In 1847 another group of Royal Commissioners arrived in Aberafan, collecting evidence about local education. They found four schools in or near the town: the National School (run by the Anglican Church and founded in 1845); Mrs. Edwards's school (1826); Mrs. Reid's school (1831) and the Margam Tinworks School (1833), which, between them all, taught some 321 children. Robert Smith was dead by now, the Tinworks had been sold to Messrs. Llewellyn, and the school is described as 'ill furnished', with an 'intelligent but untrained' master; it had 171 pupils, 65 boys and 106 girls (presumably the girls were allowed to stay at school longer than the boys who were still allowed to find work in the mines and metalworks). When he visited the National School, the local Commissioner commented that 'there is nothing like early attendance in this neighbourhood'; this was because nine a.m. was the workman's breakfast hour, so that the children had to wait until then to eat (or in some cases had to take their father's breakfast to him at the tinworks). The Commissioners were clergymen and their main interest seems to have been in the teaching of Scripture and Christian doctrine, so we learn almost nothing about what the children studied in their schools. On the other hand, if we add in the seven local Sunday Schools (which often taught reading and writing), the children of Aberafan certainly had the opportunity of enjoying at least a basic education.

All this time, as Aberafan grew from a large village into a thriving town, it had been governed by the terms of the mediaeval charter. Then, in 1832, the Reform Act was passed, extending the right to vote to all males over 21 owning or occupying a house worth at least £10 a year, and in the following year another set of Royal Commissioners visited Aberafan to enquire into the state of local government. The civic establishment had not changed since the fourteenth century, and was still made up of the Portreeve, the Constable of the Castle, various officials (haywards, aletasters etc.) all elected yearly, and an 'indefinite number of burgesses'. The senior burgesses of the Seventeenth century had now become two Aldermen, but one still had to be the son of a burgess to join the corporation.

When they described these civic offices, the commissioners also commented of the men who held them, 'the officers of the borough are farmers and labouring men, almost entirely

Public Hall buildings, Water Street. The advertisement for Olivers' shoe shop dates from 1909 – the firm still has a shop in the Town Centre.

ignorant of the English Language'; the Portreeve was 'a farmer, aged 60 years'. Oddly enough, when they came to list the occupations of the inhabitants of Aberafan, the commissioners stated that there were 76 families employed in trade and manufacture, and 45 employed in other occupations – but none in agriculture! The population was 573 – 299 men and 274 women, and of these only 5 men owned or occupied houses worth £10 or more, and were therefore entitled to vote.

The years following this report saw the building of the new docks, the coming of the railway (in 1850) and the quadrupling of the population (2,380 in 1851), milestones echoed in the building of the first Town Hall in 1826-36, and the first covered market in 1848. Newcomers arrived from North and West Wales, from the West Country and from Ireland (fleeing the Great Famine – only to run into the worst ever local cholera epidemic, in 1849). Naturally, what had suited the small, close-knit community of burgesses for so long did not satisfy these newcomers, and they began to agitate for civic reform. In 1853 a Municipal Enquiry was held, and Sergeant Wright (in charge of the local branch of the new Glamorgan police force) testified that some of the burgesses were illiterate, and past Portreeves had on occasion been charged with 'drunkenness and improper conduct'. Nothing happened at once, but in 1861 the borough obtained a new charter and the old Portreeve and his fellows gave way to the new Mayor, Aldermen and Councillors. (In fact, despite the many criticisms of their abilities, the burgesses and their descendants continued to play a leading role in civic affairs; but now the newcomers too were able to contribute their experience and management skills to the running of the borough.)

In 1861, when the new borough came into being, Aberafan was still smaller than either Taibach or Cwmafan, but whereas they were almost at the peak of their prosperity, the ancient borough was still at the beginning of its development. In the century that followed it was to become a centre of world-wide importance.

Chapter 6

The Years of Growth

There is a view of Aberafan published about 1875 which gives a very clear picture of the town at that time, some fourteen years after the new borough of Aberafan came into existence. On the east bank of the river one can see the Lower Forge Tinplate Works and South Parade (next to the present site of St. Agnes's Church), but no Station Road, and only the lanes that would become Oakwood Street and Forge Road – indeed, no buildings at all except for the occasional farm or cottage. On the west bank one can see a cluster of houses and the original Tabernacl Chapel (recently demolished), roughly where the motorway now crosses Cwmafan Road; then, moving down river, one can pick out Ebenezer Chapel, Carmel Chapel and St. Mary's Church, and beyond them the smoking chimneys of the various tinplate works built in the previous ten years. Behind this narrow strip of settlement the open land of Aberafan Burrows stretches away to the sea. It is not easy to make out any significant details of the town, but the way in which St. Mary's Church dominates the other buildings shows just how small these were.

This, of course, was the new St. Mary's Church. The original building never recovered from the ravages of the Great Flood of 1768, and in 1857-9 it was taken down and rebuilt. Many of the older members of the congregation were unhappy about this, and if there had been enough room, they would almost certainly have preferred to leave the original church standing and build a new one nearby (as was done a few years later at Baglan). However the arched frame of the east window of the old St. Mary's was built into the north wall of the new church, and if one looks at the size of this (the main window of the old church) and compares it with those in the present building, it gives some idea of the contrast of scale between the old town and the new one.

Many of the houses clustering around St. Mary's in 1875 were still thatched (though newer streets tended to be tiled or slated),

High Street, Aberafan, showing Maypole Corner

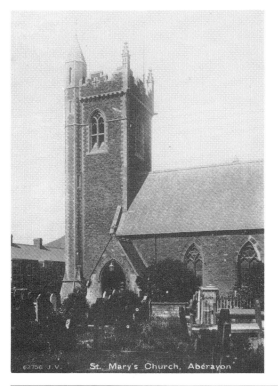

The new St. Mary's Church, with St. Mary's Place (demolished 1974) beyond

(Photographs by courtesty of Mr. Bryan Hughes).

and the town was overwhelmingly rural. Even the street names echoed this: Butter Street, Duck Street, Cattle Street, possibly the now unidentifiable Sheep Street. Pentyla had only seven houses, one of them a toll house and gate (West Gate – hence West Gate Street and West Gate Row, the cottages at the foot of the Causeway). There was an East Gate too, across the river, where Bethany Chapel now stands; this gate suffered in 1843, during the Rebecca Riots, when the gate itself was destroyed and the toll house windows were smashed and the toll keeper and his wife abused.

At the extreme left hand side of the 1875 picture one can just see a train on the main Swansea to Cardiff line, and, just beyond it, what is probably part of the docks. These, rather than the cattle and sheep of previous centuries, were to be the keys to Aberafan's future. Apart from the Margam Tinplate Works (which were technically just outside the town), there had been no industrial development in Aberafan itself until the eighteen sixties. Then, in 1864, the Margam works passed from Messrs. Llewellyns to the ownership of R.B. Byass and Co., and this marks the beginning of a period in which a succession of works were built inside the borough: the Avon Vale Tinplate Works in 1866; the Mansel Tinplate Works in 1873; and the Burrows Tinplate Works in 1874. Another, rather more exotic, works came into being in 1872, when T.E. Jones and Co. opened a tobacco factory in Water Street; it operated until 1908, thus establishing a tradition still followed today by J.R. Freeman and Son, cigar manufacturers. (At one point, in 1886, T.E. Jones and Co. processed tobacco grown locally, on the Margam estate, but the experiment was abandoned, due to tax problems; however, they did produce their own set of cigarette cards c. 1900 – a series on Welsh rugby internationals.)

Naturally this industrial expansion demanded an equal expansion in other areas such as housing, public services and transport. Curiously enough, much of this was associated with Sir Arthur Pendarves Vivian, an industrialist whose own works was based at Taibach (though he did own a brick works on Aberafan Burrows). When the new borough was set up in 1861 Vivian bought a considerable amount of land from the old burgesses, and a number of the streets later built on this land were named after his family; they included, among others,

T.E. Jones
& Co.'s
tobacco
factory,
Water
Street,
1872-1908

The Byass
Works
(successor
to the
Mansel
Tinplate
Works),
1972

Vivian Terrace, Row and Square (the latter two now demolishd), Dunraven Street, Adare Street, Wyndham Street, Dalrymple Street, Gerald Street and so on. There were suggestions then and later that the burgesses, inexperienced in high-level financial dealings, squandered what should have been the borough's resources, selling the land too cheaply. Whatever the truth of this, it is interesting to see how the names of the mayors of the new borough bear witness to the gradual inclusion of new blood, substituting surnames like Whitelaw, Smith, Daniel, Jenkins, Walsh, Stokes, Goslin and Byass for the constant Jones, Thomas and David of the portreeves and early mayors. Meanwhile a gas works had been built, and a drainage system for the town was installed in 1868-9. Perhaps this latter amenity was one reason for the ending of the regular series of cholera outbreaks; the worst of these was in 1849 and the last in 1866 when, in Aberafan alone, at least seven people died of the disease. (The first hospital in the area was the cottage hospital in Penycae Road, now two private houses; it was built by Miss Talbot of Margam Castle in 1892-3.)

In past centuries Aberafan had been to a large extent cut off from its nearby valleys by poor road links; the people of the Afan Valley had looked to Neath or Maesteg or even the Rhondda rather than to the little town at the mouth of the Afan. Now that too was to change. The growth of industry in the valleys had led to the building of tramways by which coal, iron ore and finished metal products could be brought down to the harbour, but these links were becoming inadequate, and in 1885 the Rhondda and Swansea Bay Railway opened its first stretch of line, from Aberafan to Cymmer. This was extended through to the Rhondda in 1890, and soon it became clear that Port Talbot Docks would have to be considerably enlarged in order to deal with the amount of traffic now available. Hence in 1894 the Port Talbot Railway and Docks Company was set up, to enlarge and modernise the Docks and to open up a railway link with the Llynfi and Garw valleys (both coal-producing districts). Once again the Talbots were involved, as was the Earl of Dunraven (A.P. Vivian's brother-in-law) and Colonel Wright, of Wright, Butler and Co., the steel company, and the reconstructed dock was opened in 1898. This new harbour could deal with the increased volume of exports and imports, but it also attracted industry down from Cwmafan, first the steel works and then the copper works, which were rebuilt at the dockside. It also drew the coal-trade from Porthcawl (which became a holiday resort instead).

Oddly enough, in view of this expansion, the eighteen nineties were a period of depression as far as the local metallurgical industries were concerned. This was largely the result of the McKinley Tariffs of 1891, American protectionist laws meant to help their own steel industry to get established. The Margam and Avon Vale Tinplate Works both closed, as did a number of the other local steel works, and in 1901 only eighty men were employed in the iron and steel trade here (though seven hundred and seventy-eight were employed in the tinplate works). Fortunately the harbour and the railways came to the rescue (for the first, though certainly not the last time); also in 1901 two hundred and ninety-three men were engaged in engineering and eight hundred and thirty-five in rail and transport; another seven hundred and ninety-three were employed in the mining industry. (The population of Aberafan in 1901 was 7,553.)

The new railways not only carried coal and steel, they also provided passenger services. There were usable roads now too, so that the people of the valleys could get to Aberafan Beach without difficulty. The beach had not been developed at that point, apart from the building of the Jersey Beach Hotel, and photographs taken c. 1900 show long stretches of inviting sand backed by dunes almost as impressive as those at Merthyr Mawr. The photographs also show bathing machines (for the more timid or modest bather!), swing-boats, donkey carts and various huts and stalls selling teas, fruit and refreshments. It was an ideal spot for Sunday School trips, which would come down by train to Port Talbot Central Station and then transfer to horse-drawn brakes for the last part of their journey; passengers on the Rhondda and Swansea Bay Railway could use the Aberafan Seaside station. Naturally the railway companies were not slow to recognise the possibilities in this, and began to lay on special trains. On June 20th, 1887, for instance, the R. and S.B. ran special trains to Aberafan to see the celebrations of Queen Victoria's Golden Jubilee, complete with a 'grand display of fireworks by Messrs. Brock and Son' and the ceremonial

The Jersey Beach Hotel and Promenade

Aberavon Beach and the Old Breakwater, between the two World Wars
(Photographs by courtesty of Mr. Bryan Hughes)

opening of the 'new road to the sea beach', Jubilee Road (renamed Victoria Road in 1901).

Once upon a time the beach may also have been the haunt of Bando players. Bando was a form of hockey played between neighbouring parishes, and the Margam team was famous, but their poet laureate, author of the song 'The Margam Bando Boys', was Thomas Bleddyn Jones, who lived near the Causeway, Aberafan, and no doubt Aberafan Beach did duty as a practice field for the local boys. However it was too boisterous for later Victorian opinion and in 1876 it was overtaken by a new game when the Aberavon Rugby Football Club was formed. The club was disbanded in the early eighteen eighties, but refounded in 1887, since when it has gone from strength to strength, picking up its nickname, 'the Wizards', on the way. Soccer dates from a little later when English and Scottish workers employed on the reconstruction of the docks in 1894-8, began to play matches, and cricket also owes its local arrival to industry, being introduced by Captain Robert Lindsay, manager of the Vivian Copper Works.

Sport was one form of recreation, but not everyone wanted to spend their leisure time chasing balls round muddy fields. The Victoria Institute was opened in 1887 and its facilities included a library, while many of the chapels organised socials, concerts, penny readings and other cultural activities; but these too were not everyone's choice. Happily there were plenty of less strenuous or less earnest activities to be enjoyed. Circuses and fairs were regular visitors, bringing all kinds of exotic sights to the peaceful streets of Aberafan – lions, tigers, bearded ladies – attractions that brought the inevitable entry in the school log: 'Circus visited town. Great drop in attendance!'. Slightly less exotic, though equally exciting, were the travelling theatre companies, like those run by the Haggars or the Cwmafan based Ebley family. Sometimes these companies would put on their plays in a suitable building – a barn, perhaps, or a market hall – but many places were closed to them because they were regarded as not entirely respectable, so they also carried their own portable theatres with them. (It is not too surprising that they were seen as dubious characters, since the plays they performed were mostly melodramas like 'East Lynne' or 'The Murder in the Red Barn', or light comedies like

'Mother-in-Law' and 'Is Marriage a Failure?', performed for Miss Talbot and other local dignitaries in November 1899.) The travelling theatres were usually set up in the Aberafan Cattle Market, on Water Street, and many a mother took her youngsters to see the actors in all their glamour, slipping in quietly, not quite sure if she was doing something disgraceful or not. After 1900 the theatres slowly gave way, first to travelling cinemas and then to fixed buildings like the Ebley family's Olympic cinema in Cwmafan.

There were, of course, two other forms of entertainment available to the people of Port Talbot at this time: the chapel and the pub. One can speak of the chapel as a place of entertainment without disrespect, because in the years between 1850 and 1950 chapels were not only spiritual centres, they also promoted a wide range of activities, from amateur dramatics and choral singing to Sunday School outings and 'youth clubs' such as the Band of Hope. This was quite deliberate, intended to provide a respectable alternative to such things as theatre-going or, perhaps worse still, visiting the cinema. The Band of Hope was particularly intended to combat the enormous increase in public houses and general drunkenness towards the end of the nineteenth century, and it has to be admitted that though temperance sometimes became a little too intemperate for its own good, its cause was worthy. Industrialisation had its negative side, and it was all too easy to find escape from the pressures of unemployment, large families and drab surroundings in the depths of a bottle.

By the turn of the century Aberafan had almost as many chapels as public houses, and both reflect the history of the town in their names or membership. Carmel, Capel Moriah, Ebenezer, Tabernacl, Bethel, Zion, Bethany, Wesley – Presbyterians, Baptist, Independents, Bible Christians, Primitive Methodists – families from Aberafan, Carmarthenshire, Cardiganshire, Scotland, Cornwall, all settling down together. As for the public houses, they too echo the changing face of the town, from the Burgess Green and the Corporation Arms to the Forge and Hammer and the Englishman's Home. One group of names commemorates the arrival of the Irish immigrants who came to the town about 1850, at the time of the Famine. There had been Irish families in Cwmafan just

The
Walnut
Tree Hotel
shortly
before it
burned
down in
1972

From Worrall's Directory, 1875

THE WALNUT TREE HOTEL
COMMERCIAL AND POSTING HOUSE,
ABERAVON, PORT TALBOT,
MISS JONES, PROPRIETRESS.

Commercial Gentlemen and other Visitors will find first-class Accommodation at the above Establishment.

Wines, Spirits, &c., of excellent quality. A superior Billiard Table, &c.

An Omnibus attends the arrival and departure of each Train at the Port Talbot Station.

POSTING IN ALL ITS BRANCHES.

before that and the church registers note the burial of the occasional Irish 'traveller', but from 1846 onwards Aberafan too began to have a significant Irish community, and this also marked the return of Roman Catholicism to the district. (In 1676 official lists noted that there were 25 Anglicans, 4 Nonconformists and 'no papists' in the area.) At first they worshipped in their own houses, then they moved to a skittle alley alongside the main railway line, after which they rented Capel Moriah (the Baptists had moved to Ebenezer); the first St. Joseph's was consecrated in 1860. To begin with, the newcomers were mostly unskilled labourers, but they soon learned enough to become tradesmen and skilled workers, and, as such, a valued part of the community. The Hibernian Arms, the Shamrock of Erin and the Erin Go Bragh all took their names from this connection.

As the docks expanded, and auxiliary industries and businesses established themselves nearby to take advantage of the new facilities, so there also grew up a need for services such as offices, banks, specialist shops and all the requisites of a thriving seaport. Postal facilities had always been good because the town was on the main road through South Wales, but banking services took a little longer, starting in 1863 when the Glamorganshire Banking Company opened a branch office in High Street, at the house of Mr. Whitelaw, a confectioner. At first this was only open two days a week, but by 1864 the Mayor was suggesting that the company be asked to open every day except Sunday, and this was done.

At first 'Port Talbot' referred only to the docks themselves, but now, as Aberafan began to spread across the river on to th east bank, so the name 'Port Talbot' began to apply to the new business and residential streets that were built in the years from 1880 to the beginning of the First World War. Station Road was soon under construction. Bethany Chapel was opened in 1879, and the Victoria Institute next to it in 1887, while work began on what is now Glan Afan Comprehensive School in 1893. Initially the seaward side of the road was made up of ordinary dwelling houses, with little gardens in front of them, and though all of these are now shops, it is still possible to see their domestic origins. On the landward side, however the buildings were clearly designed as shops from the very first,

Civic services in the nineteenth century included some that we would not expect today. The Aberafan Borough Gasworks dated from 1869, though one Shopkeeper installed gas as early as 1844.

Electricity was a later arrival, though Margam Castle and the Abbey Church were fully electrified in 1891

with the upper floors meant for use as offices. Behind Station Road a network of streets grew up, some, like Crown Street, the work of independent builders, others, like Mansel Street, intended for the employees of particular works.

All this new building took place on land owned by the Margam Estate, and the Talbots took an interest in what was done. Hence the 'new town' had only one hotel, the Grand, built, so legend says, to look as little like licensed premises as possible. (There were also the Dock Hotel, The Pilot's Rest or Tiddlywink, and the Port Talbot Inn near the old docks; perhaps the Talbots felt that these were a necessary safety-valve for the sailors and dock workers.) On the other hand, it is said that Miss Talbot in particular was concerned to see that the new road network should be adequate to cope even with the increased traffic of future years; one only has to compare Station Road with the narrow streets and lanes of Aberafan at that time to see how important this was to prove. One obstacle, though, even the Talbots could not prevent, and that was the level-crossing on the Rhondda and Swansea Bay line which cut across the main road next to Aberafan Bridge, and caused innumerable delays for the half century or more that it was in existence.

Reconstruction in Aberafan itself was limited. Many of the older buildings were rebuilt, to cope with increased population and new standards of housing, and a number of new public buildings were put up, like the Public Hall in Water Street (first meeting place of the Afan Masonic Lodge), but short of wholesale demolition there was nothing that could be done about problems like the narrow streets and the awkward corner where High Street met Water Street. In 1907 the covered market caught fire and had to be rebuilt, opening again on March 1st, 1909; nothing so drastic happened to the old Town Hall, but it was clearly inadequate for the new bustling Port Talbot, and a more appropriate civic headquarters was planned, opening in 1915 as the Municipal Buildings. The last obvious link with the mediaeval lordship of Afan had already gone, in 1895, when the ruins of Aberafan Castle were cleared and its mound was levelled.

Yet some things were seemingly unalterable. In 1909 heavy rain caused flooding yet again, and on the night of September

Panelling from Aberafan Town Hall (1840-1934), used as a back fence in Green Park, c. 1969.

Port Talbot Municipal Buildings, 1971 (With overflow hut on roof)

28th the greater part of Aberafan was under water. The Canister Bridge was washed away, and Green Park and Lower Water Street were under several feet of water – so much so that in two houses the families had to be rescued through the roofs. Almost a hundred families suffered the loss of their belong-ings; some livestock was drowned and a number of businesses had their stock and premises damaged or destroyed, though happily this time there were no human casualties.

Something else that did not change was human nature. The inhabitants of Aberafan were not noticeably wicked, but the town's expansion did lead to a demand for some sort of police force and in 1840 John Angus, a police officer from Liverpool, was stationed in the town. One of his first successes was the conviction of three publicans 'for serving beer on Sunday during the divine service' – an interesting sidelight on both the nature of local crime and Victorian morality. In the following year a Glamorgan County Force was set up and Aberafan was allotted one constable, Peter Wright; he was later promoted to Sergeant, but as late as 1853 he was the only official policeman in the town. (The various local works also employed their own security forces who co-operated with Wright when necessary.) Eventually a police station and courtroom were built in Talbot Square (1856-7), but the force itself remained at one officer for some years after that. By 1875 it had risen to a Sergeant and three constables, and by 1898 it was necessary to build a new police station, this time for Port Talbot rather than Aberafan.

Behind the records of expansion, however – new streets, new organisations, new public services – there were always the people for whom and by whom these things were made. Aberafan had never lacked its share of unusual or gifted characters, and we have already met a number of them, like the fiery Morgan Gam, lord of Afan, or the poetic blacksmith who kept Edward Donovan awake in 1802. One such character was John Richards of Cwrt Isa Farm (in the docks area), who was appointed 'Emperor of Aberafan' in 1863. The title was traditional, a piece of folk-lore, and such 'royalty' was not uncommon elsewhere in Britain, but John Richards was notable for more than this. His other, earned title was the 'poor man's friend', and he was noted both as a successful farmer and for

71

Aberafan's first Police
Station and Court Room,
built 1856-7, in Talbot
Square

Port Talbot Police
Station, built 1898,
demolished 1971

the help that he gave, like his neighbour Robert Jones of Court
Farm, to his Irish tenants. His philanthropy was very practical;
in 1858 he was recorded as having removed ten tons of ashes
and filth from Aberafan town centre, and he was always
anxious to heal family quarrels among his tenants.

Another lively native of Aberafan was Thomas Bleddyn Jones,
mentioned earlier as the official poet of the Margam Bando
Boys. He was a printer by trade, and a freeman of the old
borough by inheritance; his great-grandfather Evan Jones,
landlord of the Red Lion, had held office as portreeve of
Aberafan on a number of occasions. Thomas Bleddyn Jones
wrote in both Welsh and English, and had a considerable gift
for satire, but he was also something of a musician (con-
ducting the Aberafan Brass Band during the eighteen fifties)
and a talented step dancer, performing both in the local
travelling theatres and at the functions of the Bando team at
Margam Orangery.

As it happened, the Margam Bando Boys were not simply
a sports team. They played under the leadership of Theodore
Talbot, the heir to the Margam estates, and since both Theodore
and his father, C.R.M. Talbot, were also keen military men,
the Bando Boys became the nucleus of the Rifle Corps
formed in 1859 (when there was the threat of a French
invasion). When the invasion failed to materialise, the
volunteers continued to meet and drill, and though much of
their activity centred around Margam, they also had a parade
ground near the river Afan (marked now by South Parade).
Occasionally they staged mock invasions of Port Talbot
Burrows or Aberafan Beach as training exercises. In 1908 the
local force became part of the Territorial Army, as the 7th
Cyclist Battalion, the Welch Regiment.

Sadly, they were soon to find themselves involved in real
battles when the First World War broke out in 1914. Since aerial
warfare was in its infancy, Port Talbot suffered no direct
attacks, but the first local man was killed in action in France
in September 1914. Meanwhile Rupert Price Hallowes,
Assistant Works Manager at Mansel Tinplate Works and cousin
of Sir Sidney Byass, had enlisted the day after war was declared;
he had previous military experience, and by September 1915
he was a second Lieutenant in the Middlesex Regiment, and

in the thick of the fighting in France. He was fatally wounded at the beginning of October, but his courage had earned him the Victoria Cross, and his example led to many local men, particularly from the Mansel Works, enlisting in the army. There are no official totals for the number of Port Talbot men killed or wounded in 1914-1918, but the various war memorials, in the parks and in churches, chapels and offices bear witness to the range and cost of their service.

Not everyone agreed with the war, however, and there were many conscientous objectors in South Wales. The most prominent of these in Port Talbot was Taliesin Mainwaring, who spoke publicly, in Bethany Square and elsewhere, and was jailed for three months as a result. (He became mayor of Port Talbot in 1924-25 and again in 1952-53.) There were other signs of the war locally; soldiers were often billeted here, and in October 1914 fifty-five of them are recorded as sleeping in shifts in the billiard room of the Grand Hotel. There were Belgian refugees too, billeted in Springfield Terrace, in Bethany Chapel Manse; they helped to bring the less glamorous side of war home to those local enthusiasts who had been attracted by war posters and recruiting drives.

While the conflict continued, the demand for munitions, tanks, ships and all the other armaments of modern war kept heavy industry at full stretch throughout Britain. Locally, the pressure fell particularly on the Port Talbot Steelworks, built in 1901-2 near the General Station, by Messrs. Gilbertsons of Pontardawe. The founder of Gilbertsons had begun his career at the Copper Works in Cwmafan over fifty years before, but this did not prove a good omen for the new steel works, which was hit by strikes; after some eighteen months of idleness they were sold to the firm which eventually became Guest, Keen and Baldwins; the first steel was rolled there in January, 1907. Then, in 1916, Messrs. Baldwins built the Margam Steelworks, to produce steel for the use of the Port Talbot operation. The new plant was at the dockside, and this finally confirmed the movement of local heavy industry away from Cwmafan and (for the moment) Taibach; Margam Moors were still the haunt of geese and sea holly.

Once the 1914-1918 war was over, industry throughout Britain fell into a slow decline, culminating in the Depression years of the nineteen thirties. Although Port Talbot was better able to face this than many other towns, because it still had such a wide range of industries within its boundaries, it had its share of unemployment – an average of 46% between 1931 and 1934. The Port Talbot Steelworks shut down for a while in 1923, other local works were also affected, and many of the collieries in the surrounding areas either closed or worked on short time. As a final blow, the dockside Rio Tinto Copper Works was hit by the effects of the Spanish Civil War, and shut down in 1937.

Naturally these years had their effect on the town. In 1926, the year of the Great Strike, local support groups were set up, like the 'Port Talbot Adult Canteen Committee', based at Bethany Chapel, and although there were no collieries in Aberafan itself, no-one could be unaware of what was happening in the villages of the Afan Valley which depended entirely on the coal industry. Less obviously, new building, both residential and commercial, had almost stopped, and apart from a few exceptions like Val D. Jones's house on Baglan Road, the residential centre of the town from Abbey Road to Beach Hill is overwhelmingly late Victorian or Edwardian in style. (When house building began again, after the Second World War, it was on what were then the outskirts of the town, at Sandfields and along Baglan Road.)

Initially, as we have seen, Aberafan and its neighbours were a number of separate villages; Baglan and Margam were very much under the control of the Llewellyns and Talbots respectively, Taibach and Cwmafan were the province of the two companies (Vivian and Sons and the English Copper Company) which had built them up in the first place, and Aberafan itself had its own borough government. However, as the years passed, this arrangement became less and less realistic. Aberafan began to spread across the river into Port Talbot, and out along the Baglan and Cwmafan roads, the two companies began to shrink and play less of a main part in the administration of their areas, and it became clear that some new arrangement would have to be made. The Margam Urban District Council had been inaugurated in 1894, with its headquarters at Taibach, and had proved very successful, but Aberafan Council had approached Margam even before that

Talbot Memorial Park, officially opened 1926, (but previously a playing field)

Port Talbot Hospital, built 1916
(Photographs by courtesy of Mr. Bryan Hughes)

with the idea of amalgamating all the local authorities into one borough. This idea continued to surface from time to time, and eventually, in November 1921, the new borough of Port Talbot came into existence, including Aberafan, Baglan, Bryn, Cwmafan, Margam, Oakwood and Taibach. (There had been a suggestion that Neath should also join the new borough, but this did not happen.) The administrative headquarters of Port Talbot were the new Municipal Buildings in Water Street, and the last Mayor of Aberafan and the first Mayor of Port Talbot were the same man, Alderman Sidney Byass; Sir Sidney (as he later became) was also the first man to receive the Freedom of the new borough, in 1925.

There was some regret that the historic name of Aberafan had been abandoned, but it was still the name of the local parliamentary constituency, and when Ramsay Macdonald, who was its M.P., became Prime Minister in the Labour Government of 1924, Aberafan was recognised nationwide.

By 1921 the population of Aberafan had risen to 15,370; Margam (which included the Station Road area) was 17,774, and Cwmafan 6,201. Baglan was still a picturesque hamlet with a population of 682. The total figure for the borough was 40,027, and one can see how the lean years that followed 1921 must have drained the area of its people; in 1965, even after the expansion that came with the building of the Steel Company of Wales (which at one point employed between 16,000 and 18,000 men and women) the population was still only circa 52,000.

Although local industry was in the doldrums between the two world wars, local sporting, cultural and social life was as vigorous as ever. In addition to rugby, soccer and cricket, the borough played host to boxing, bowls, water polo, golf and athletics. Quoits, a much older game was played until the nineteen twenties, and it was particularly popular during the strikes of 1921 and 1926 when poultry and other useful prizes were presented to the winners; the teams were mostly attached to public houses and played in a West Wales League. There was motor-cycle racing at Aberafan and Margam, and in 1928 the local swimmers organised a long-distance swimming club which regularly entered for the Mumbles-Aberafan swim. Port Talbot sportsmen were successful on the

The Majestic (also known as the Odeon), Forge Road, 1972

The Grand Cinema, High Street, 1971

wider stage too, and Billy Beynon the boxer was only the best known of a number of champions produced in the borough.

Perhaps the most colourful of all these sporting characters was Percy Hunt, the 'Great Marvello'. If any one had decided to choose a typical Aberafan family the Hunts could have fitted the bill in almost every particular, except that they were not of burgess stock. Percy was born in Tymawr Street (also known as Butter Street – the narrow road leading from High Street into Talbot Square); his mother came from Cornwall and his father, Thomas, from Devon. Thomas Hunt was first a miner (at the Morfa colliery) and then a tinplate worker, until a leg injury left him driving a horse and cart from the market square to Aberafan Beach, carrying visitors in the summer and any available cargo in the winter. He was also Aberafan's last town crier. By now Port Talbot had a number of Music Halls and cinemas; Vint's Palace of Varieties in Water Street was one of the earliest, and in 1921 Leon Vint also opened the New Theatre in Talbot Road. The Public Hall in Water Street was used for concerts, but in the nineteen twenties and thirties boxing matches were put on there, and Percy Hunt would perform his strongman act between bouts. He also performed at Vint's Palace and the New Theatre, and at the Picturedrome in Taibach; in the early days when he had hardly any weights, he would use his younger brothers and cousin instead.

As time went on, the music halls tended to show films rather than variety acts, but there were also purpose built cinemas: the Grand and the Capitol in High Street, the Electric in Forge Road (built, 1914, demolished 1949), and the more recent Majestic (1939 – later the Odeon) and Plaza (1940). Even in the Depression years most people were able to afford the price of at least an occasional cinema ticket, and so escape from their daily problems into the glamour of a Hollywood musical. Meanwhile, for those who preferred to make their own entertainment, the town was rapidly building up a fine tradition of amateur dramatics and music, with the Port Talbot Operatic Society, the Cymric Glee and similar groups, and with the drama group associated with Leo Lloyd and the Y.M.C.A. which ultimately produced such fine actors as Richard Burton and Anthony Hopkins. There were discussion groups

**Signs of the coming
conflict, 1938**

too, and University Extra-mural and W.E.A. classes for those whose interests were more academic. The students in these classes could make use of the new Aberafan branch library, opened in 1936, as well as the library of the Victoria Institute. And behind all this there were Sunday School outings, fêtes and fayres, Whit Walks and teas, jazz bands and carnivals and all the home-made entertainment of a community too lively to be crushed by economic gloom.

Unhappily, when an upturn arrived, it was once again the result of war. This time the town did not escape so easily, and though the lie of the land, with the mountains so close to the sea, meant that enemy bombers could not inflict the kind of havoc on Port Talbot that they did on Swansea, they did succeed in doing some damage. Six civilians were killed in Sandfields on February 14th, 1941, and on the following May 12th four people from Pontrhydyfen were killed (this included the family of the singer Ivor Emmanuel). Fortunately the death toll among those in the Armed Services was much less than that in the 1914-1918 War, but there were one or two fatal plane crashes locally, and at least one ship was blown up by a mine as it left the harbour.

This was a more visible war, of course. Barrage balloons floated overhead, there were bomb craters and demolished houses to be seen, and even if the enemy planes rarely succeeded in doing serious damage, they and the search-lights that tried to pinpoint them often made an aerial display as beautiful as it was deadly. Housewives had to cope with rationing and the blackout, and those men who were not eligible for military service found themselves joining the Home Guard or carrying out firewatching or A.R.P. duty. In a very real sense, the front line in this war was at every household's front door.

Not everything that happened between 1939 and 1945 was to do with the war, though most things were drawn into it. For instance, the two new cinemas, the Majestic and the Plaza, were soon showing such morale-boosting films as 'Mrs. Miniver' or 'The Foreman Went to France'. And when Margam Castle was sold in 1942, it was soon being used for the billeting of troops, both British and American; strange accents and foreign uniforms added a note of the exotic to the streets of Port Talbot. At last the fighting came to an end, and V.J. Day, August 15th,

1945, saw a grand celebration of the final victory of the war, with bonfires everywhere hailing the return of light after so many years of darkness.

Almost immediately after the war was over, Port Talbot found itself launched into a new project. The area had always been in the forefront of advances in steel technology, and now it was selected as the site for one of the first integrated steel works in Britain. Guest, Keen and Baldwins had already carried out some preparatory planning before the war, but when the Steel Company of Wales was formed in 1946 (from G.K.B., Richard Thomas and Baldwins, John Lysaght and Llanelly Associated Tinplate Companies), the building of the new works went ahead with the utmost speed. The site chosen was Margam Moors; it was flat, near a modern port, and with good access to supplies of limestone and coking coal. At that point environmental considerations (the loss of the dunes and marshlands and their flora and fauna) were second to the needs of industry – though the claims of history were acknowledged when the new strip mill was named the Abbey Works. (According to local tradition, the Works has its own ghost, one of the monks of Margam Abbey.) Meanwhile, the older Margam Steelworks was remodelled, new coke ovens were built, and new handling equipment was installed at the docks.

The various portions of the new Works began production during 1950-51, and on July 17th, 1952, there was a grand ceremonial opening of the hot-strip mill, with Hugh Gaitskell, the Chancellor of the Exchequer, as the guest of honour. This was not the end of development at the Works, however; they continued to be modernised and extended throughout the nineteen fifties and their scope was even further increased when the associated Trostre and Velindre Works were opened at Llanelli and Llangyfelach respectively.

The Port Talbot Steelworks, overtaken by the new technology, closed down in sections between 1952 and 1961; and in 1962 the docks ceased to export coal, so that they could concentrate on the needs of the iron and steel trade. Even this was not enough to cater for the new generation of iron ore carriers, vessels so huge that their braking distance was twenty miles or more, and the Steel Company of Wales was soon involved in planning and building a new Tidal Harbour

Port Talbot
Docks
shortly
before
closure,
1971

One of the
last Ships
to use the
Docks,
1971

to accommodate them. This was duly opened by the Queen on May 12th, 1970. (The old docks closed down altogether the following year.)

At this point the prosperity of the town was such that outsiders called it 'Treasure Island', but the opening of the new harbour probably marked the high point of Port Talbot's fortunes to date, and the harbour itself has in many ways been the saviour of the town during the recurring recessions of the 70s and 80s. In these years the Steel Company of Wales has been first nationalised, and then privatised, as well as being subjected to such a drastic streamlining that its total of employees fell from c. 16,000 to c. 4,000. Initially the works produced such a bountiful harvest of rates and other income for the borough of Port Talbot that it was able to plan developments like the Afan Lido and Sports Complex (1965) and the new Aberafan Centre (1976) and Civic Centre (1986), but the economic downturn has meant that further development is on temporary hold.

Although the new Steel Works drew its work force from all over south-west Wales and beyond, many came to settle in Port Talbot, and there was the need for a great deal of extra housing to accommodate them and their families. Hence the building of the new works on Margam Moors was parallelled by the building of a vast new council estate on the sand dunes behind Aberafan Beach, which inevitably became known as Sandfields. At first this 'instant community' had something of the slightly forlorn air of all new towns (the flatness of the site and the sandy soil did not help), but as time went on and young families were born and grew up on the estate, Sandfields became a genuine neighbourhood, complete with schools, churches, shops, pubs and clubs. It was even, for a short period in the late seventies and early eighties, the administrative centre of the borough, since temporary council offices were put up next to the Afan Lido during the construction of the town centre.

The first stage at Sandfields had to be erected fairly rapidly but the estate has continued to develop ever since. Prefabricated housing put up at the end of the 1939-45 war was eventually demolished to make way for more permanent homes; more recently an industrial estate has come into being on the moorland between Sandfields and Aberafan, and at the western end of the estate B.P. Chemicals (whose Baglan Bay plant first came on stream in 1963) have gradually extended their works into one of the most modern and sophisticated examples of its kind.

As for Aberafan itself, the last twenty years have seen the greatest transformation in its entire history. The first stage of this was the construction of the motorway that now swoops across the roofs of the town. We have already seen the importance to Aberafan of its place on the main east-west route across South Wales, but by the middle of the twentieth century the town was sabotaging its own advantages. First there was the infamous level crossing in Station Road, but even when that disappeared with the closure of the R. and S.B.R. line, there was the dire hazard of Maypole Corner (where High Street met Water Street); this had been a problem even in the days of horse-drawn traffic, but as cars and lorries grew ever larger, the problem became a potential disaster. Sadly, the narrow strip of land between the mountains and the sea left very little room to manouevre when it came to planning a bypass, and many landmarks disappeared to make room for the new road. Capel Moriah, home to so many of the religious denominations of the town, was one of the victims, as were Vivian Square and Carmarthen Row. The motorway was opened in July 1966, just in time for the Royal National Eisteddfod, which was held at Margam that August. (The Eisteddfod had previously visited the town in 1932; its junior version, the Urdd Eisteddfod, visited Port Talbot in 1983.)

The clearance needed to make room for the motorway was only the beginning. In 1971-2 most of what was left of the original town of Aberafan was demolished, so that work could begin on the Aberafan Shopping Centre, a modern indoor shopping mall, part of which would replace the old covered market. The centre, which was opened by the Princess Royal on February 20th, 1976, covers that part of Aberafan which lay between High Street and the main railway line, but the demolition also took in that land on the far side of the railway which is now the bus station and car park, as well as Margam Terrace (now the site of the open-air. market) and part of Bethany Square. More recently the new Civic Centre (on the site of the former Talbot Square) was brought into use in March 1986; it was officially opened by the Princess Royal on September 29th, 1989. An inner ring road, Heilbronn Way, had already taken through traffic out of the centre of the town, and now Station Road and Forge Road, between Glan Afan Comprehensive School and St. Agnes Church, were pedestrianised, linking across Aberafan Bridge with the elegant paved square and fountain outside the Civic Centre.

Meanwhile there had also been changes in local government, and on April 1st, 1974, a new borough came into existence, uniting the old municipal borough of Port Talbot and the Urban District of Glyncorrwg. At first the new borough adopted the name of Afan, acknowledging both its long history and the inclusion of the Upper Afan Valley within its boundaries. However this proved somewhat unhelpful for non-natives (who confused it with Avon, Bristol) and it was decided (not without some regret) that it would be more practical to revert to 'the borough of Port Talbot'! (One interesting sidelight here is the number of councillors who were in some way descended from, or related to, the burgesses of Aberafan; clearly a tradition of public service had been established.)

Nowadays of course, the civic authorities no longer dispense justice, though the local magistrates' courts were housed in the Municipal Buildings until traffic noise from Water Street and the nearby railway, combined with the lack of adequate accommodation, made it necessary to move elsewhere. The Forge Road Swimming Baths (opened 1900) were empty, following the opening of the magnificent pool at the Lido, and so in March 1969 they were taken over as temporary Magistrates' Courts; later the General Offices of the Port Talbot Steelworks were adopted as a permanent home for the administration of justice. (It did not prove possible to find a new use for the Baths, which remained empty for some time before being demolished in September 1991.) The reorganisation of the South Wales police force also doomed the original Port Talbot police station (built 1898), which was no longer adequate, and a new headquarters was put up on the same site, opening in 1973.

Despite all these drastic changes, certain things remained the same. For instance, on November 12th, 1972, the Afan burst

The Byass Works (Mansel Tinplate Works)
The engine house, Port Talbot Steel Works, 1971

its banks yet again, and though no-one was drowned, the resulting mud and slime were quite as much of a misery for the five hundred households affected in Aberafan as they had been in 1607, 1768 or 1909. (Though recent work on the river bed and banks do give some hope that the long tale of flood disasters is finally just a memory.) But if 'Treasure Island' has become 'Giro City' for many in recent years, Aberafan still has enough resilience to be sponsoring an annual Community Festival to celebrate the town's achievement, past and present.

One wonders what John Leland, writing of the 'poor village of Aberavon' in 1550 would make of it if he could see that same 'village' today, or what Robert Smith would think of the new Carmel Chapel and the Abbey Works, or Caradoc ap Iestyn of the civic centre that has replaced his castle as the focal point of the town – or even what we today would think if we could see the Aberafan of 3000 A.D.! Of one or two things, though, I suspect we can be reasonably sure: that there *will* be an Aberafan – and somewhere in the town there will be a descendent of the burgesses of Afan helping to run it!

Chapter 7

The Vanished Town

Aberafan from Gwarycaeau, 1875

High Street

High Street

High Street

Church Street

High Street

The view from Aberafan Bridge

Riverside Views

Cwmafan Road

Cwmafan Road

Cwmafan Square

Cwmafan Square

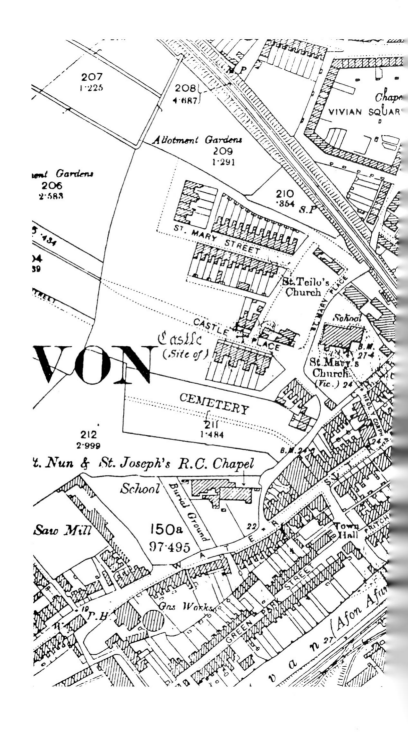

von c.1899 The town still has a cattle market, and the site of the castle is marked

Water Street

Water Street

Water Street

Water Street

Heol y Corph

Water Street

Bethany Square

The Casino Club

Arcade, Muncipal Buildings

Vint's Palace of Varieties

Pritchard Street

The Public Hall, 1972

St. Mary's Place

Water Street and Heol y Corph

Town on the High Road

Water Street

Clarence Street

The Arcade, Municipal Buildings

Water Street

Demolition of the Walnut Tree
after a fire, 1972

Aberafan Working Men's Club

Aberavon Station, 1971

Clarence House (Borough
Housing Department)

Station Road

The Plaza Cinema, 1939 (Courtesy of Plaza Film Theatre)

St. Mary's Church, c.1850 (Notice the outside staircase to the gallery; this was a much plainer, more countryfied church, with white-washed walls, and high-backed pews for the congregation.

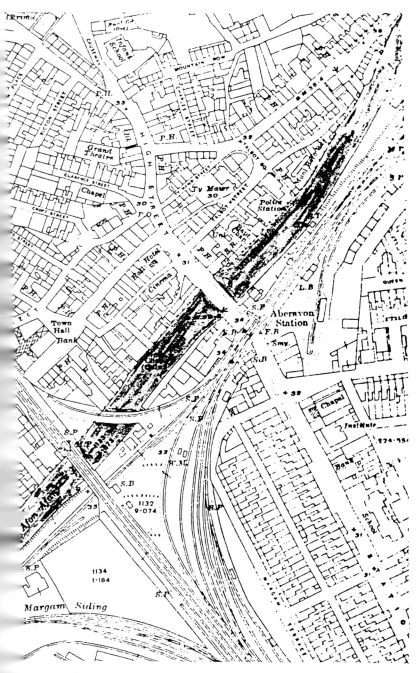

von c.1917 The new Town Hall and Arcade are open, and the first cinema is marked

Carmel Chapel, c. 1890

1971

Capel Moriah; home to Baptists, Independents, Catholics, Wesleyans and the Salvation Army.

Water Street English Baptist Chapel

Bethany Chapel 1880 (still in the open fields)

Tabernacl Independent Chapel,
Cwmafan Road

Port Talbot Synagogue, (now the
Spiritualist Church)

Wern Independent Chapel

Groes Village – demolished 1975